T0149579

From an Immigrant's Oven

Unclench your fists when you pray for peace.

From an Immigrant's Oven

A Casserole of Our Family's Potted History from the Vantage Point of My Stomach

by

ARTHUR GARDINER

with Illustrations by

GARRY 'SASQUATCH' PECK

Recipes and anecdotes from our family's nomadic past, with a plethora of inappropriate aphorisms and useless trivia

---

Cure For Mange On Dogs:

10lb lard; 1lb sulphur; $1^1/_2$ cups kerosene; $1^1/_2$ cups vinegar. Melt the fat, add the ingredients in the order given above, and store in a wide mouthed jar. Wash the dog, apply the mixture liberally all over.

TRUE DIRECTIONS | iUniverse®

AN AFFILIATE OF TARCHER PERIGEE

FROM AN IMMIGRANT'S OVEN
A CASSEROLE OF OUR FAMILY'S POTTED HISTORY
FROM THE VANTAGE POINT OF MY STOMACH

iUniverse books may be ordered through booksellers or by contacting:

iUniverse
1663 Liberty Drive
Bloomington, IN 47403
www.iuniverse.com
1-800-Authors (1-800-288-4677)

Because of the dynamic nature of the Internet, any web addresses or links contained in this book may have changed since publication and may no longer be valid. The views expressed in this work are solely those of the author and do not necessarily reflect the views of the publisher, and the publisher hereby disclaims any responsibility for them.

Any people depicted in stock imagery provided by Thinkstock are models, and such images are being used for illustrative purposes only. Certain stock imagery © Thinkstock.

ISBN: 978-1-5320-1245-7 (sc)
ISBN: 978-1-5320-1244-0 (hc)
ISBN: 978-1-5320-1243-3 (e)

Library of Congress Control Number: 2016920069

Print information available on the last page.

iUniverse rev. date: 12/16/2016

"Not everything that counts can be counted, and not everything that can be counted counts." Albert Einstein

---

DEDICATION

Pour toute la famille, particulièrement Bo et Colm, grâce à qui ce travail a été nécessaire et possible.

To all the family, especially Bo and Colm, who made this job both necessary and possible.

Aan alles van die gesin, besonder Bo 'n Colm, wie het hierdie werk nodig 'n moontlik wees.

Life's greatest mystery is how that boy, who wasn't good enough to marry your daughter, is now the father of the smartest grandchild in the world.

INTRODUCTION

Somewhat bedraggled, after surviving vicious civil wars, dragging our unwanted butts from one country to the next, one continent after another, some of our family only finally landed in Canada in the 1980s and 1990s. We're a mongrel tribe, whose Scots and Belgian, with a sprinkling of English and Swiss, antecedents hit Africa in the late 19th and early 20th centuries: some of whom built businesses or farms; others, mines from raw bush. Another part of the clan, the Ukrainians, skedaddled from Eastern Europe between wars, coming directly to Canada.

Some of us suffered the ignominy of being stateless refugees, some lost citizenship, some our culture, our language: we all lost our homes. But, we survived; welcomed, to our surprise, by our new compadres. Some stayed in eastern Canada; some of the family came west. Originally, I compiled the recipes for the family, lest they lose their heritage entirely; but I was urged to share our past misfortunes with other Canadians, so they, too, can laugh at them.

Whence came the recipes? Many were from my mother's and grandmother's stained and dog-eared cookbooks; many evolved with the family, as recipes do; others I gleaned from the travels that my job entailed. Are they original? Some are, but many come from scraps of paper and the backs of my technical notebooks, linked to some weird reminiscences.

And to you Canucks who were here to welcome us so warmly: "Merci, eh!" and "Bon appétit", and "Enjoy."

Arthur Gardiner
2016-10-10

I've changed most folks' names, to protect the guilty.

A $\frac{1}{10}$ inch slice of wine cork stuck behind the base of a picture frame will prevent a dark line on the wall paper...you'll get a circle instead.

...some of our family only finally landed in Canada in the 1980s.

> "Never attempt to teach a pig to sing: it wastes your time and it annoys the pig."
> **Robert Anson Heinlein**

After existing for two weeks on a diet of tacos and beans in Honduras, at the first restaurant we reached as we came out of the bush, near Choluteca, we ordered their house specialty: grilled tilapia with baked potatoes and all the trimmings. Talk about fresh! As Gustavo and I enjoyed a couple of ice cold beers, the patrón *dropped a line in his well-stocked pond beside the kitchen, while his spouse collected spuds, herbs and vegetables from the garden.*

CONTENTS

I have observed that at almost every meal where there is convivial company, the discussion at table always turns to food; not only about the current meal under examination and consumption, but also of meals past, meals to come, restaurants visited, restaurants to be visited, recipes tested and tasted, recipes untried.

Why? Perhaps because the soul of a human is in his stomach.

Honey Sauce

In a double boiler, melt 2oz butter, stir in $^3/_4$ cup honey, pinch of cinnamon and grate in a hint of nutmeg. Good on pancakes.

CANDIES

At the tender age of seven I was consigned to a boarding school that was very similar to Hogwarts, without the magicians. Ah, what a school that was: up at six every morning; sprint down, bare-bummed, to the outdoor pool, summer and winter for a quick couple of lengths; then back to the dormitory to change for matins and one class before breakfast. They tried, mostly unsuccessfully, to turn us into young English gentlemen by beating an appreciation for literature, the classics, religion and the love of God into our bums with a birch cane.

There, I was ever envious of all my peers, whose 'tuck-boxes' were always filled with 'shop-bought' candies; while I had to make do with what my doting mother and grandmother had made for me. My peers, in turn, were all insanely jealous of the fact that my family took the time to make candies for me; whereas their parents had merely turned the task over to a mail-order factor.

What follows in this section are samples of my mother's, my grandmother's and my great grandmother's recipes.

Cure for Smoker's Cough

To cure a persistent cough, my mother recommended a dose of Epsom salts to her friend, a pack-a-day smoker. When her gullible friend tried the prescribed medication, it did cure the cough, temporarily. Her friend was too nervous to cough, in case she "spilled the beans", as my mother put it.

The friendship soured thereafter.

1

Easter Eggs

These were always a big hit! They aren't difficult to make, merely finickity (that's granspeak *for finicky-pernickety).*

Requirements:

    1 egg per child plus 1 egg per adult
    Adult eggs are served as soft boiled eggs.
    Kids' eggs are made as below.

Instructions:

    Make a hole about twice the size of a match head in the blunt end of a raw egg, then using a straw, blow the egg. This means you blow into and across the hole very gently, and the guts of the egg comes out. Be sure you get it all out, then wash the inside of the egg thoroughly and dry it.

That was the easy part!

    The difficult part is to fill the eggs. The easiest is either Turkish delight or marshmallow, both of which are poured in as a liquid, from the recipes below.

My father was shy, serious and straight-laced; mother was anything but. At cocktail parties she always made some trick canapés: among the delicate ham sandwiches, you could be sure there would be one where the ham was replaced by a carefully trimmed triangle of pink surgical lint. On a plate of sausage rolls, at least one would be filled with the cork from a wine bottle, or popcorn that squeaked when bitten. A carefully crafted marzipan mouse often found its way into our tuck boxes, to our delight and the dormitory matrons' horror.

To Peel A Hard-Boiled Egg.

Prick a tiny hole in the blunt end of a raw egg. Boil for 7 to 10 minutes. Plunge into icy water to chill, leave for a minute or more. Crack the shell and it will peel perfectly every time, immediately, or hours later.

Turkish Delight

Traditionally, these are flavoured with rose water: now there's a challenge. Collect a very large quantity of roses, strip off the petals, then steam them. Alternatively, buy a bottle of rose water from a Middle Eastern shop. It's a prime export from Persia (Iran).

Requirements:

2$^1/_2$ cups sugar $^1/_2$ cup gelatine

1 cup icing sugar   1 cup corn flour

1-2tblsp rosewater *(depends on quality)*

$^3/_4$-1 cup water *(or cheap rose water, then you don't need flavouring)*

Instructions:

Put sugar, rose water and gelatine into pot, heat, stirring as you go, until all sugar and gelatine are dissolved. Boil for about 10 minutes, then add colouring and flavouring. Pour into shallow square metal baking tray. Liquid should be about an inch deep. Leave to cool and set.

Put icing sugar and corn flour into brown paper bag, shake thoroughly (*keep bag tightly shut, or you'll be covered*). Tip about a quarter of bag's contents onto a sheet of wax paper and spread out thickly. When gel is cool and fully set, dip bottom of tin into hot water briefly, then flip onto the waxed paper. Tip next quarter of bag's contents onto top of the gel, and spread around. Slice gel into cubes by dipping blade in hot water. Put all cubes into paper bag and shake them around to get them coated thoroughly with icing sugar/corn flour.

My mother's great friend, Helena, was Greek. Because of the traditional enmity between Turkey and Greece, she could never call this anything but its Greek name, loukoumi.

A philosophical question.
How can a guinea-pig show he's pleased, if he hasn't got a tail to wag?

> **"If it quacks like a duck, and it walks like a duck, it needs another five minutes in the microwave." Me**

Coconut Ice

No kids' party was complete without coconut ice. Although there is no difference in taste, the best was always two-tone pink and white. Helena made it green and purple once, but we refused to eat it because it looked gross.

Requirements:

2 cups sugar $^1/_2$ cup milk

1 cup desiccated coconut

Instructions:

In a double boiler (which is very important, or you'll burn the milk) mix milk and sugar, heat and boil for 3 minutes without stirring. *If you stir, the sugar will crystallize out very rapidly.* Take off the stove and stir in the coconut. Turn out onto a lightly buttered tray, lined with wax paper. Repeat, but put cochineal in the second layer: it looks nifty! When completely set, cut into 1 inch squares.

Although we lived in the tropics, coconuts were an exotic fruit for us, because the country was high altitude and land-locked. For some strange reason, no-one ever thought of growing pineapples or bananas on a commercial basis in the country either, so they were also exotic and rather expensive.

We had bananas growing behind the house on the mine, but although we obtained lots of fruit from them, they were regarded with suspicion, because the banana grove housed a thriving rat and frog population, both of which attracted snakes.

Garnish Vert-Pré: Grilled Meats

Bunches of water cress (or some call it garden cress) with a mound of crisp julienne French fries, served with a dab of *maître d'hôtel* butter or *café-de-Paris* butter on the meat.

Watermelon Konfyt

At first appearances, this is goofy: throw out the meat of the watermelon and keep the rind. However, one can eat the meat! Just keep the rind to make the konfyt.

Requirements:

1 watermelon.	12 cups cold water
2 tblsp calcium hydroxide	$^1/_4$ cup fresh ginger root
Equal weight of sugar to the weight of the rind	

Instructions:

Cut open melon, scoop the guts into a bowl. Smoosh this up to get juice, strain and toss pulp

(*alternatively, eat the melon, and forget about the juice*).

Peel green skin off white rind. Toss skin; keep rind. Cut rind up into $^1/_2$ x 1 x $1^1/_2$ inch chunks, prick with a fork. Mix calcium hydroxide into water, toss in rinds and leave steeping 12 hours. Drain rinds, wash with fresh water, then boil in water for about 20-30 minutes. Meanwhile, put sugar in another pot; add juice plus water to equal about 3 cups of liquid per cup of sugar.

Now comes a very brief fun part.

Put ginger in muslin bag, whack it several times with mallet to get it thoroughly bruised, chuck bag into sugar-juice, mix and heat to get sugar dissolved.

Drain rind, drop into sugar-juice concoction and simmer gently until rind is clear and translucent.

Either bottle with syrup, or remove rinds, let them dry and keep in a tin in the crystallized form.

No question: weird as it may sound, this is really the best use you can make of a watermelon.

Garnish Vert-Pré: White Meats And Duck

Green peas, French beans and asparagus tips, mixed in melted butter. Served with clear gravy.

Fudge

I have never admitted this to my dear mother: she always made sure we had a good supply of fudge in our tuck...but I really didn't like it. Rather than appear an ingrate, I accepted courteously, then traded it at school for "shop-bought" candies. I had much the best of the deal, as I traded two squares of hazelnut fudge for a Mars bar.

Requirements:

2 cups sugar	2tblsp cocoa
1tblsp butter	1 cup whole milk
$1/_2$ cup chopped hazelnuts	$1/_2$ cup raisins or sultanas

Instructions:

Mix everything but nuts and fruits in double boiler, then simmer until mixture hardens when dripped into cold water. Stir in hazelnuts, raisins, sultanas, pour into well buttered dish and cut into 1 inch squares.

At high school, there was always some entrepreneurial kid out to make extra pocket money. Some were the school barbers, some traded stamps, some were cracker-jack anglers, selling their catch. Then there were the fudge makers, who did a roaring trade. One particular lad, Stan, had a secret method of boiling unopened cans of sweetened condensed milk, to form the most incredible caramel. Alas, one day when his attention strayed doing homework, one can blew up, coating his study with a sticky brown residue that looked like the contents of an exploded diaper. Save for his dignity, Stan was relatively unharmed, but his confectionary career ended abruptly.

In Brazil, at the mine near Ouro Preto, Marta, the cook in the Casa Grande, made a dessert called doce de leite *that tasted very similar to Stan's fudge. She made it by slowly simmering sugar and milk until it set. Did she add anything? I never did discover, but I think not.*

Raw And Cooked Eggs

Spin an egg on the counter, then stop it, and release immediately. If it stays still, it's cooked: if it starts to move again, it is raw.

his attention strayed... one can blew up, coating his study with a sticky brown residue... like the contents of an exploded diaper.

Marshmallows

Nothing store-bought quite equals the exquisite taste and consistency of home-made marshmallows, of which I have fond memories. The candy dates back to the time of the pharaohs, from whom my family probably learnt it (it's been in the family that long).

Requirements:

$^1/_2$ cup cornstarch	$^1/_2$ cup frosting sugar
3tblsp gelatine	$^1/_2$ cup cold water
2 cups berry sugar	$^1/_2$ cup light corn syrup
$^1/_2$ cup hot water	$^1/_4$ tsp salt
2 eggs	1-5tsp rosewater*(depends on quality*

Instructions:

Grind gelatine in pestle and mortar to fine flour, then sprinkle over cold water in large bowl. Leave to soften. Mix together frosting and cornstarch in brown paper bag. Line base of baking pan with waxed paper; lightly oil, dust bottom and sides with part of frosting-starch mix. Heat berry sugar, corn syrup, and hot water gradually, stirring constantly, to dissolve sugar, then bring to boil, without stirring, for about 10 to 12 minutes. Remove from heat, add rosewater, pour over gelatine mixture, stirring until gelatine dissolves. Whip briskly until volume triples and mixture thickens ±10 mins. Separate the eggs. Beat whites and salt until stiff. Fold into sugar mixture until just combined. Pour into baking pan; dust with frosting-starch mix. Chill until firm (3-12 hrs). Run knife round edge of pan; invert onto cutting board. The concoction should just drop out; remove waxed paper. Cut into 1 inch cubes, then shake with remaining frosting-starch mix in brown paper bag to coat completely.

Café-de-Paris Butter

Knead 4oz butter with $^1/_2$ tblsp chopped parsley, $^1/_4$ tsp salt, good pinch of coarse ground pepper, juice of 1/4 lemon & 1 full bulb crushed garlic.

Mebos

When we were children, Christmas was never white, nor a blizzardy festival, with chestnuts roasting on an open fire. December is midsummer, when it is as hot as Hades, made almost pleasant by constant monsoonal rainfall. That was when we were treated to inexpensive high quality imported South African fruit, such as peaches, nectarines, sweet brown-green hanepoot *grapes and apricots by the tray. But best of all was the* mebos, *the dried salty-sugary apricot candy. As kids, we were very strictly rationed on this delicacy, because too much had disastrous effects on our digestive tracts.*

The recipe is simplicity itself!

Requirements:

Equal quantities (1 lb) dried apricots and berry sugar.
Salt to taste replacing an equal amount of sugar.
(the salt makes it interesting)

Instructions:

Wash, but do not soak the apricots. Dry then mince them thoroughly. Keep about $1/2$ cup sugar to one side, then mix the apricots thoroughly with all the remaining sugar and salt, and pass through the mincer again. Knead the mixture well, then spread onto sugared waxed paper. Cut to 1 inch cubes Roll in berry sugar to coat the cubes.

The etymology of mebos *is a testament to the eclectic nature of Afrikaans: It comes from the Japanese* umeboshi *which refers to* dried salted ume *plums. The basis of the language is Dutch, but the word for furniture is* meubels, *from the French* meubles; *the word for jerky is* biltong, *which comes from Malay. Tangerines are* naartjes, *from the Portuguese* naranja *for orange.*

Paw Chewers

To stop a dog chewing his paw, put oil of cloves or tea tree oil on the spot he's chewing.

FDR Candies

These were good standbys for our tuck-boxes, but it took me a while to figure out why mother insisted on limiting my intake. In a way, they are another take on mebos. Where and when the recipe originated is not hard to guess: the dirty thirties in USA. When I asked her why they are called FDRs, my grandmother grunted: "They get things going again." The ingredients may also have had a part in the name.

Requirements:

1lb dried figs	1 lb pitted dates
1lb raisins or sultanas	$^3/_4$ cup berry sugar
salt to taste	

Instructions:

Mix fruit together in a large bowl, sprinkle with salt, put it through mincer, mix again, and mince again. Shape into thumb-joint sized balls; roll in berry sugar.

Peanut Squares

These peanut squares were great trade goods; but, as I rather fancied them myself, the counteroffer had to be quite substantial.

Requirements:

2 cups hot roasted peanuts	1 cup sugar
$^1/_2$ tsp bicarbonate of soda	salt to taste

Instructions:

Melt sugar and salt in iron skillet, stirring to prevent burning. As soon as sugar melts, stir in bicarb then mix in peanuts, remove from heat and pour quickly onto buttered, waxed sheet on baking tray. Roll out smooth and cut immediately into squares.

Quick Sauce

Heat $^1/_2$ cup each of water and golden syrup; add $^1/_2$ oz butter, a pinch or 3 of ground ginger, zest of 1 lemon. Excellent on pancakes.

Almond Crescents

These are not actually from my mother. I don't recognize the handwriting on the faded scrap of lined paper, but it is very precise. My guess is that it comes from Linda, the daughter of one of the neighbouring farmers. She was the head sister at the obstetrics ward at the General Hospital, who should have become matron by right of seniority, but political correctness and affirmative action required that the position go to a black lady, several rungs down the ladder. The unfairness must have hurt Linda deeply but it never affected her friendship with the woman.

Requirements:

1 cup salted butter	$^1/_3$ cup berry sugar
1 cup flour	$^2/_3$ cup ground almonds;
$^1/_3$ cup chopped almonds	

Instructions:

Mix together dry ingredients except chopped nuts, then gradually work in the butter by rolling back and forth on a floured pastry board. When fully mixed, roll out onto waxed paper, cut with cookie cutter into crescents, sprinkle with chopped nuts. Bake in slow oven until golden yellow, but do not brown, as they then taste awful! Why crescents? Why not?

In Brazil, Marta, the cook on the mine at Passagem da Mariana made much the same candy using cashews instead of almonds. No breakfast in Brazil was complete without a glass of juice from the cashew fruit, which is grey, wet and sweet, with an astringent aftertaste: not the greatest gastronomic experience.

*Cashew is a strange fruit, bearing a single nut encased in a poisonous oxalic acid impregnated shell **outside** the fruit that looks like a golden-orange capsicum (Aussie-speak for sweet bell peppers).*

Glacé

Beaten egg-yolk brushed over cream buns or éclairs then sprinkled with berry sugar before baking makes a fine gleaming finish.

BAKING

In Kansas I was confused when the breakfast waitress offered me biscuits and gravy with my bacon and eggs. In the British idiom, a biscuit is what north Americans call a cookie; what you call a biscuit is a scone to me: the last thing I wanted for breakfast is a cookie, certainly not with a fried egg, least of all with gravy poured over it. Next morning there were hot cakes for breakfast. By then, being slightly more educated, I assumed these were also scones. Wrong! They're pancakes. The tea that I ordered with my breakfast was iced, not hot. I found that pop is what teenagers drink, not the sound a weasel makes in a nursery rhyme; a flat is a punctured tyre (tire with a Y), not somewhere to live; a bonnet is an outmoded ladies' head-dress, not the sharp end of a car; the nether end of which is the trunk, not boot.

MUFFINS, SCONES AND BISCUITS

Tex-Mex Biscuits	13
30 Day Bran Muffins	14
Lemon Muffins	15
Scones	16
Griddle Cakes	17
Pancakes	18
Crêpes	20

There is a sea food restaurant chain in North America which has an excellent advertising and marketing division; but, at every location at which we have dined, the service is atrocious, food mediocre, ambiance unexceptional and the prices barely acceptable.

Why do we return, when our every visit confirms these criticisms? Because they serve the same, most exquisite hot, fresh savoury scones with every meal, at every location.

Heinlein's advice on raising kids
Don't handicap your children by making their lives easy.

Tex-Mex Biscuits (or Scones if you prefer!)

Requirements:

2 cups flour	1 tblsp baking powder
2$^1/_2$ tblsp soft unsalted butter	1 cup grated cheese
$^1/_2$ cup medium or hot salsa	1 cup ice cold water
pinch salt	and other things

Measure ingredients precisely, then add a bit. All ingredients are ±50%!.

Instructions:

Preheat oven to 400°F. Lightly spray baking tray with Pam, dust with flour, bang out excess on a pile on kneading board. Mix together all dry ingredients. Using your hand (preferably, but not necessarily, washed) rub in the butter. Dough should be dry, but stick together with light compression. Mix in cheese, which should have a bit of bite. Use provolone, parmesan, emmental or aged cheddar. Add salsa and water, stir rapidly, then dump onto thickly floured board.

My own preference is for aged cheddar, but not so aged as to have green mould growing on it, or that it tries to climb out of the bowl. 'Mild' salsa would work, but it's too colourless to give anything like the right 'oomph', 'very spicy' generates bleats from wimps, so use medium.

Dough should be soft enough to work, but stiff enough to form single cohesive mass. Sprinkle flour on the top, flatten, fold in half and half again, flatten, repeat and flatten again until 1 inch thick. Cut with cookie cutter (or whisky tumbler); place on lightly greased then floured baking tray. Place midway in oven. Bake 12 minutes at 400°F; change oven to broil for further 2 minutes.

Serve hot with butter (or crispy bacon or sausage).

Chinese Cuisine

For really good Chinese food, go to a Chinese restaurant. Unless you're ethnically Chinese, you can't make it half as well as they can: MSG is in their DNA.

30 day Bran Muffins

Here's one from a really close relative: Wendy, the second cousin once removed of my brother's wife's sister-in-law. Hers is an interesting tale. Her husband, who is as wide as he is tall, built of solid muscle even now as a septuagenarian, played professional league rugby as a young man. They won their house in a lottery some 40 years ago.

Wendy hates washing up, so she uses only disposable plates, cutlery and dishes. Hence, a word for the kitchen garbage bin has crept into the family lexicon: "Wendy's Dishwasher".

Requirements:

2 cups Demerara sugar	2 cups flour
2 cups bran	2 cups milk
$^1/_2$ cup cooking oil	2 eggs
$^1/_2$ tsp salt	1 tblsp bicarb
1 cup chopped dried fruit	

Instructions:

Beat eggs and sugar enthusiastically in an old ice-cream pail, add everything else and beat well again. Close the tub; put in the fridge overnight or over a month. Drop as many as required into greased paper pattipans. Bake at 350°F for 12-15 mins.

The wonderful advantage of this method is that you only have to wash the spoon used for beating, unless you use a disposable wooden paint stirrer as a spatula like Wendy; everything else goes into the garbage, which is a typically Wendy-esque touch.

Their front room is papered with a forest scene on one wall. Instead of a chesterfield, there's a park bench, which fits perfectly.

Ripening Avocados

When buying avocadoes, go for Hass rather than Fuerte variety. They ripen and taste much better. Buy them green. To ripen, simply place in a brown paper bag in a cool cupboard for a couple or four days.

Lemon Muffins

These evolved for our then adolescent daughter who disliked plain scones, would not eat Wendy's muffins because "they're gross, full of diseases from that ratty ice cream pail", and was fashionably lactose intolerant, so could only eat dairy in "mac 'n cheese" and ice cream.

Requirements:

2 cups flour	$^1/_2$ cup Demerara sugar
2 tsp baking powder	pinch of salt
$^1/_4$ cup soft, unsalted butter	1 egg
zest of a lemon	ice cold water
juice of a lemon	

Instructions:

Preheat oven to 400°F. Lightly butter muffin tray, dust with flour, invert and bang out excess flour. Sift together all dry ingredients, then rub in butter. Consistency after adding butter is critical. Mixture should seem dry, yet stick together when compressed lightly in the hand. Make well in dry mix, into which add the lemon zest, egg and enough water to make a smooth, but not sloppy mixture. Finally, add lemon juice, beat briskly for a few seconds, then pour into pans and bake for 10-15 mins. Top of muffins should be tanned, not pasty pale. Turn out hot onto wire cooling rack. Eat within 2 hours, or they'll be stale.

When we meet at the local café someone often brings muffins, despite a sign: "NO OUTSIDE FOOD OR DRINK". When a youth asked why the manager was evicting him, not us, we overheard her reply:

"Yes, they're loud and obnoxious: and yes, that is outside food. However, they've spent a lot of money on coffee here every day over the years. I need their custom and loyalty more than I need yours. Get out, get over it and get a life!"

Corks

If a cork is too large, don't trim it, boil it for a minute, and it should slide home like a homesick gopher.

"Life is like a sewer: what you get out of it depends on what you put into it."
Charles Castelin

Scones

This is the only baking my brother ever learnt when we were kids. As teenagers, when we were hungry, he'd bake a batch of scones, whether for breakfast, lunch or dinner. My mother was a scone aficionada; a true expert who bullied anyone who deviates from her original recipe...however, as she never actually measured the ingredients when she was making them, it is difficult not to stray from the straight and narrow, and more difficult to know when that occurs.

Requirements:

2 cups flour	4 tsp baking powder
4oz unsalted butter	pinch of salt
milk, buttermilk, sour milk or water	

Instructions:

Sift dry ingredients into a bowl. Rub in butter. Now comes the difficult part, for which I'll quote her verbatim: "add enough liquid to reach the right consistency" (!?!). Pat out lightly onto floured board, dust top with flour; fold, then refold, flattening dough and re-dusting each time. Cut into "pieces of the right size" (*I use a glass tumbler as cookie cutter*) and bake in quick oven (450°F) for about 10 minutes.

These have to be served fresh. Split in half, and served with a pot of lemon curd, or buried under fresh whipped cream and strawberry jam, these are to die for! They evoke wonderful memories of Sunday afternoon tea at Cockeye House, my grandparents' original quirky homestead on Longview farm. The house started as two thatched inverted tanks, with a window and door cut into each; then the area between was bricked in as a sitting room; gradually... toilet... pantry... bathroom... kitchen... veranda... dining room... scullery were added.

Au Jus

Means "with juice", so to serve some *"with juice"* in a gravy boat is just plain pseudo-intellectual garbage. What is served in the gravy boat is "*jus*": what is served with it, on the plate, is served "*au jus*".

Griddle Cakes

I learnt these in the Yukon from our field manager, George, who could do anything, but was always too honest for his own good. When Barbara, his wife, asked him: "Do these jeans make me look fat?" George was dumb enough to respond: "It's not the jeans, dear."

Requirements:

$^1/_2$ cup flour	2 eggs
$^1/_2$ cup sugar	$^1/_4$ cup milk
$^1/_4$ cup cooking oil	4 tsp baking powder
$^1/_4$ cup water (use $^2/_3$, and if too stiff, add what's left)	

Instructions:

Mix together flour and sugar. Beat eggs, milk, oil and water and beat into flour mix. Lastly, beat in baking powder, and leave to stand for 30 mins. *Do not stir after setting aside.*

Drop large spoonfuls onto lightly oiled, hot griddle, turning when bubbles rise. These should be about 1 inch thick when done. Split them open and serve hot with butter.

Before the computer age, and the wonders of GPS, George embarked on his brother-in-law's ketch to sail to Hawaii. The brother-in-law's navigation skills were such that when they reached Tahiti, George refused to sail further and flew home. And the brother-in-law? He made it safely to Tasmania, where he sold the boat, but never did see Hawaii.

George is the only person I know who has worked both north of the Arctic circle, on the Polaris mine; and south of the Antarctic circle, putting in an airstrip for the Brits on South Georgia. An avid fan of Ernest Shackleton, the Antarctic explorer, he cooked up a penguin stew while he was there. When I asked him how it tasted, he replied:

"It's penguin. Don't matter what you do to it, penguin always tastes like bloody penguin!"

Household Hint

When making mayonnaise, use a splash of the vinegar from pickled beets to give it a pretty pink colour.

Pancakes

Our first surprises on arrival in western Canada were the free pancake breakfasts every day for the ten days of the Stampede, all over the city. Somehow, the pancakes and bacon stirred nostalgic memories of the old country, and we all wept with homesickness. Standing before the meerkat exhibit at the Calgary zoo evokes the same response, which had other zoo patrons staring strangely at the four of us weeping quietly.

Requirements:

2 cups flour	2 tsp baking powder
milk, buttermilk, or sour milk	1 tsp sugar (or not)
1 oz unsalted butter	1 egg and a pinch of salt

Instructions:

Sieve together and mix thoroughly dry ingredients, then beat egg and completely melted butter into a cup of milk and add to dry mix, beat and add more milk until you have a smooth liquid batter, but not too liquid. Heat griddle and lightly oil. Pour 2 tblsp of batter onto skillet, then another separate dollop, then another. Each pancake should be about 4-5 inches across and $\frac{1}{2}$ inch thick. Bubbles will rise through batter. Let them burst, and as the holes begin to become permanent, flip the pancakes. That took about a minute and a half. Cook other side for the same time. Oil up the griddle again by wiping with an oiled paper towel. Repeat for the next 3 pancakes: you should get 2 to 3 dozen from the quantities given. Keep warm in a paper towel wrapped in a kitchen towel.

The cook in our exploration camp, Debbie, made pancakes with Saskatoon berries that she had picked herself. They looked great; but tasted of Deet with which she covered herself for the black flies.

Cleaning Windows

When cleaning windows, do it vertically on the outside, horizontally on the inside. Then you know when you missed a spot.

Somehow, the pancakes and bacon stirred nostalgic memories
of the old country and we all wept with homesickness.

> "The sea is only the embodiment of a supernatural and wonderful existence."
> Jules Verne

Crêpes

Nothing says French cuisine quite like crêpes for dessert, yet they are so simple to make.

Requirements:

1 cup flour	2 tblsp brown or white sugar
1$^1/_2$ cups milk	pinch salt
4 eggs	4 oz butter

Instructions:

Melt butter, and beat into milk and eggs. Sieve dry ingredients (with or without 1 tblsp sugar, brown or white) together into mixture, whisking vigorously. Tip about $^1/_4$ cup of batter into lightly buttered medium hot 12 inch skillet, and spread with flat wooden spatula to cover bottom of skillet. Cook for about 3 mins, then flip and cook about 1 min more.

Remove crêpe from skillet, sprinkle with brown sugar and a pinch of cinnamon if desired, then roll tightly and keep warm in a tea towel. Serve with a squeeze of lemon.

As a refugee family after we skedaddled, man, wife, two young kids and a dog, living for months in two rooms in a boarding house, with a small (illegal) hotplate and skillet, we made these crêpes as one of our first meals in the new country. Ah, such inexpensive luxury!

We had little money, but every Saturday we bought a beer each, and the kids had a pop; until the day when money was really tight, so we decided to skip even that treat. The kids mutinied, standing before us with their mugs, waiting for their pop. Of course, we had to get 2 beers and the cans of pop. Who wouldn't?

To Relieve Mosquito Bites

To relieve mosquito bites, use vinegar;
To relieve mosquito bites, rub on meat tenderizer;
To relieve mosquito bites, rub on lemon juice;
To avoid mosquito bites, don't get bitten.

> "A nice creamy chocolate cake does a lot for a lot of people; it does for me."
> **Audrey Hepburn**

CAKES AND THEIR ILK

I'm something of a traditionalist, who does not believe in the benefits of "eating healthy", nor in following a "palaeo-diet"; which sounds as if it requires you to run out and whack a woolly mammoth every time you're hungry. Therefore, when my wife and my daughter suggested I include in the book such weird creations as zuccini cake, kale and cabbage muffins, spinach bread and carrot cake, I rebelled. Not only would I not eat such aberrations myself, but I would not inflict them on anyone else in the world. More importantly, they do not come from any recipe books in our family. My mantra is simple: "vegetables is vegetables, cakes is cakes: don't mix the two".

Accordingly, my response was a simple Aikona, Até, Nyet, Nien, Nee, Nie, Non, Não *and No, which covers "No" for most eventualities.*

Really useful hint

During the wet season in central Africa, always, *always*, iron all your clothes, especially underwear. It kills the *putsi* fly eggs, and thus prevents their maggots burrowing into your skin.

Whereas I come from a line of bakers, my spouse's family culinary arts focused on the range, not the oven. However, she quickly rectified this to become a dab hand at baking with a decidedly French accent.

Beignets (which is a sort of French doughnut)

This is the recipe for the second best beignets in the world. The best are at the Café du Monde in New Orleans, where they have been serving beignets and coffee since before the war of 1812!

Requirements:

$^1/_2$ cup homo milk	$^1/_2$ cube yeast
2 cups flour	2 egg yolks
2 oz unsalted butter	$^1/_4$ cup berry sugar
1 tot rum (or to taste!)	1 tblsp lime zest & juice
vanilla essence to taste	pinch or two of salt.
1 cup frosting sugar	1 cup cornstarch

Instructions:

Mix yeast with $^1/_4$ cup warm milk, $^1/_2$ cup flour & 1 tblsp sugar. Cover with towel and leave in warmth to rise (*$^1/_2$ hour: volume doubles*). Mix egg yolks, sugar, salt, rum vanilla, lime juice and zest in double boiler. In separate bowl, beat melted butter into balance of milk, then mix all in with yeast dough. Cover with towel and leave in warmth to rise again (*$^1/_2$ hour*). Knead lightly, roll into 2 oz balls, place 1 inch apart on floured baking tray, leave to rise for 1 hour. Deep fry at 350°F, turning every minute for 4 mins until golden brown. Rest 1 minute, then dust liberally with frosting-starch mix.

After spilling the sugar dusting on the floor, we apologized to the guy cleaning up at Café du Monde, but he just grinned and said:

"No problem, man. That's what's guarantees my job security."

Greener Boiled Beans

A pinch of bicarbonate of soda added when you boil green beans keeps them bright green.

Chiffon Sandwich Cake

My mother turned these out like an automaton for bake sales and the like. I remember her entering two identical cakes of this recipe in two separate sections in the home industries competition at the local agricultural show...and winning first prize in both sections! My brother and I were fed the flops - he ate the frosting, I ate the cake - but they were few and far between.

Requirements:

1 cup flour	$^3/_4$ cup sugar
lemon zest	3 tsp baking powder
$^1/_2$ tsp salt	$^1/_4$ cup cooking oil
3 eggs	$^1/_2$ cup water

Instructions:

Grease and line with paper 2 x 8 inch cake tins. Preheat oven to 350°F. Sift together in bowl #1 all dry ingredients except salt. Separate the eggs, putting yolks in a cup, to which add lemon zest, oil and water and whisk briskly. In bowl #2 beat egg whites and salt until stiff. Fold flour mixture into the egg whites until just mixed. *Do not stir or beat.* Pour into tins, place in oven. Bake for 20-25 mins at 350°F. Remove from oven, leave in tins for 5 mins, then run a knife around tin and invert. Cool on a wire rack.

My wife never had success because the centre always sagged. So it was I who made the cakes for bake sales: until the day a sale was sprung while I was away on contract. Always game, she tried, but flopped as ever, so she propped up the sunken centre with an inverted saucer, intending to buy the cake herself, and thus hide the deception. Alas! Someone else bought it...and she was too embarrassed to 'fess-up. Our tea service has been a saucer short ever since.

Household Hint

When all else fails, read the instructions.

"Make the most of what you yet may spend, before you too, into the dust descend." Omar Khayyam

---

The 'Only' Chocolate Icing

The birthday cakes my mother made for us as kids were the stuff of legends: the decorations were the envy of every child at our school. Whereas theirs were mundane, dreary "shop-boughts"; ours were home baked masterpieces: automobiles; farmyards; rugby, cricket and soccer fields. The talent has skipped a generation, but now our daughter creates fantastic and credible monkeys, dachshunds, skydivers and 'Habs" logos. They have one common factor: her chocolate icing.

<u>Requirements:</u>

$^1/_3$ cup soft unsalted butter $^1/_3$ cup cocoa

2 cups frosting sugar   2 tblsp milk

1 tsp vanilla essence

<u>Instructions:</u>

Work butter into dry ingredients until smooth; add vanilla and beat thoroughly. Add milk a little at a time, mixing as you go until smooth and workable. Apply with a metal spatula, dip in hot water periodically to ensure a good even spread.

When decorating, *keep it simple.*

A smooth, polished finish is done with a hot wet metal spatula. Alternatively, create a choppy sea, using a snappy flick of the wrist. Another attractive texture can be made using a 4 tine fork, either tracing quarter circles, or making a sort of tangle of curls, like a poodle's hair.

When I was a young man, Antonio, a Portuguese sheet metal worker on the mine, made the most amazing bouquets of roses, tulips, dahlias, ferns and carnations, from old oil cans and braising rods! He'd originally apprenticed as a confectioner in a bakery, then applied exactly the same principles to making iron flowers, after he learnt to weld.

Kicking Fruit Salad Up A Notch

Add a tot of dark rum and the pulp of two passion fruit to the bowl just before serving.

Boston Bread

This was a regular feature of our afternoon teas on the farm, served with a slathering of thick rich farm butter. I always imagined it was an American favourite as well, but I have only encountered it once on this continent, in the Yukon, made by Debbie, the camp cook.

Requirements:

1$^1/_2$ cup dates	2 tblsp butter
1 cup brown sugar	2 tsp bicarb
2 cups boiling water	3 cups flour
3 eggs	1 cup walnut fragments

Instructions:

Mix together dates, sugar, nuts, butter and boiling water. Set aside to cool. Sieve together flour and bicarb with a pinch of salt, stir this and beaten eggs into the mixture. Bake 1 hour in moderate oven (350 to 400°F)

Debbie had a parrot, whose sole repertoire was to whistle the entire theme from the Andy Griffith show, endlessly, ad nauseam. *Small wonder the woman was a couple of bricks short of a load, as that tune pretty soon drove most of us dilly, and the parrot nearly ended in the soup. Next season, when we were working in Nunavut, her parrot was banned.*

When I was working in Para, northern Brazil, I was told the recipe for parrot stew.

Place parrot under large rock in stew pot, add water and diced vegetables. When rock is tender, throw away parrot and eat rock.

Such a fate would have been too good for Debbie's bird.

Caviar

If you're wealthy, spread the caviar liberally on a slice of melba toast and moisten with a squeeze of lemon. If you're like us, spread it sparingly on a corn flake. If you're really poor, don't buy caviar.

> **"We learn from experience that men never learn anything from experience."**
> **George Bernard Shaw**

Meringues

Even winter is so hellish hot in the tropics that one could equate it to a prairie summer most of the time; so heavy meals and heavy desserts were not something we ate. The standard dessert on the farm was fruit salad, which was generally a selection of citrus, plus passion fruit, papayas and whatever was in season, like guavas, mangoes and melons. My mother would never serve fruit salad without meringues.

Requirements:
   2 egg whites
   $^1/_2$ cup berry sugar
   pinch of salt
   pinch of cream of tartar

My sister-in-law, a prize poultry farmer, insists that, if you can get them, you should always use the whites of duck eggs for meringues, as they are stiffer when beaten. I hate to admit it, but she is right.

Instructions:
   Thoroughly oil a baking tray, wipe, then dust with flour. Beat egg whites with pinch of salt until really stiff, add 2 tblsp of sugar, and beat again until stiff. Lightly fold in remaining sugar. Drop 1 tblsp dollops of mixture onto baking tray.
   Bake on middle shelf in very slow oven (200°F) until dry and brittle, say about 4 hours, when they should lift easily from the tray. Cool on wire rack. Store in airtight container lined with paper towel.
   These really are an elegant dessert, which can be served alone, or joined together with whipped cream for something really decadent. But best of all, serve them as my mother always did; as a side to a bowl of fresh fruit salad of pineapple, grapefruit, orange, papaya, melon, mango.

Quince Sambal

Mix together 1 grated quince, 1 grated onion, salt and pepper, 1 tsp brown sugar and 1 tblsp cider vinegar. Excellent with cold roast beef sandwiches. *Substitute unripe pear for quince if not available or pricy.*

Economical Meringues

My grandmother, a frugal highland Scotswoman, always made what she termed "economical" meringues. I'm not sure that the cost was that much less, in fact I'd guess that it was higher, as raising poultry and selling eggs was a big part of the farming operation. However, she called them economical, and that is the name that stuck.

Requirements:

1 egg white	1 cup berry sugar
2 tblsp boiling water	pinch of salt
1 tsp vinegar	2 tsp baking powder
1 tsp vanilla essence or lemon zest	

Instructions:

Beat egg white with salt until very stiff, add essence, zest, vinegar, sugar and boiling water and keep beating until thick, add baking powder and continue beating for about a minute, drop teaspoonfuls onto a greased baking sheet at 2 inch intervals. Bake 20 minutes at 250°F, then switch off the oven and leave at least 2 hours, or better yet, overnight. Store in an airtight tin.

For childrens' parties, one can substitute the lemon zest and vanilla with one or more teaspoons of cocoa powder, or put in some cochineal (pink and orange) or blue, yellow or green food colouring. Just go easy on it, as pastel shades are fine, but gaudy colours are out.

Great grandfather's gateaux were legendary...except on a Saturday morning when he was a little the worse for a dram at the Fairview Pub on Friday night. Then the decorated cakes were psychedelic nightmares of Antoni Gaudí colours.

Meat On A Camping Trip

When you're off camping, without a fridge, instead of buying steaks, buy a sirloin roast and rub it down with boracic powder before you leave. It will stay fresher much longer. Slice into steaks as needed.

Meringue Pie Crust

This is perfect for a lemon meringue pie topping, but use the economical meringue for the base of a New Zealand fruit Pavlova, for which there is a recipe below.

Requirements:

    2 egg whites
    2 tblsp castor sugar
    $^1/_2$ tsp cream of tartar

Instructions:

Beat egg whites with cream of tartar until frothy, then gradually add sugar, beating enthusiastically until stiff and glossy. Pile meringue on top of pie, making sure the edges are sealed. Bake at 400°F for 8-10 minutes until delicately browned.

Cool gradually in a warm place away from drafts.

A tip: turn off the oven and leave pie in it with door open, to dry the meringue. If meringue is not properly cooked and dried it will begin to sweat, and will reduce itself to a gooey sludge.

My mother always managed to burn the tips of the meringue.

Soon after we arrived in Canada, Debbie, the cook in our northern exploration camp, was constantly plagued by guys stealing her pies left out in the warm generator tent to cool and dry. Seeing a shadow on the tent wall and hearing a pastry thief at work, she charged out to beat the tent wall with a broom, screaming blue murder at the felon. A shaken black bear escaped at a terrified gallop, never to reappear, while an equally petrified cook disappeared into the kitchen, never to re-emerge (at least for a week).

To Prevent Soggy Pies

Brush the lower pie crust all over with white of egg, then allow to dry before adding the filling.

A shaken black bear escaped at a terrified gallop, never to reappear, while an equally terrified cook disappeared into the kitchen, never to re-emerge.

Pavlova

The Kiwis and Aussies argue fiercely over who invented this decadent dessert, named in honour of an early 20th century Russian ballerina, Anna Pavlova. I have heard variously that it comes from Germany, the south of France and Tahiti; even you Americans claim it as your own, as with everything.

Who really cares? Just enjoy it, and forget that it comes from down-under, up-over, or where-ever.

Make a single circular economical meringue (see above) about 8-10 inches in diameter on sheet of waxed paper on lightly greased baking tray. Edges should be slightly raised to form central saucer. When it cools, strip waxed paper and start.

Requirements:
    2 cups "old-fashioned" whipping cream
    1 tsp icing sugar
    sliced fresh fruit such as peaches, pears, apricots, mangoes, pineapple, kiwi and blue, rasp-, straw-berries.

Instructions:
    Place meringue on flat serving platter. Whip cream with sugar until very stiff. Fill cream into meringue saucer. Cover with fruit and berries. Serve and enjoy.

This is a perfect "deck" dessert to round off a summer barbeque. It is simple to make, looks exotic and tastes "divine". Cousin Gaynor introduced us to it at her childrens' birthday parties, when she was always careful to make three: two to feed the "gannets", as she called the kids, and one exclusively for the adults.

Destinking A Skunked Dog

If your dog has argued with a skunk, don't use ketchup to clean him, it's too expensive. Use dilute (50:50 with water) vinegar and soap.

Pastry

About fifty percent of what was consumed by us as kids was "recycled" leftovers. As adults, the same proportion survives, but alas, no longer as the excellent pies and tarts made by my mother and grandmother. To make any kind of tart or pie you need a really good pastry, of which there are several species. Handle as little and lightly as possible, keep it cold. Use butter or lard not vegetable shortening.

I originally wrote four pages of unadulterated garbage here, explaining how to make pastry for under-crusts and over-crusts, flaky, puffy and crumbly. However, when my spouse read it, she vetoed it:

"It's boring, and all your pastry always tastes like cardboard anyway. This is the twenty-first century: get with the times."

She suggested that it would be a lot easier to buy the frozen pastry dough from the supermarket. Like everyone else, that's what she does, so that's what you should do.

Pies are the finest disguise for leftovers, and if the pastry is made well in advance, the creation of these culinary masterpieces becomes simplicity itself.

Christmas for our family is never Christmas without the mince pies and open mince tartlets our grandmother and mother made. We were always in awe of these wonders, until my mother let slip how simple they are to make: a jar of Festive mincemeat from the local grocer, a tot of brandy for the mincemeat, another for the cook, a flat of pastry, cut oversize with a cookie cutter to fit the shallow tartlet trays, and Presto! Gastronomic perfection. For variety, strawberry jam or lemon curd replaced the mincemeat, or the top crust was replaced with meringue topping.

Vinegar, The Wonder Drug!
A cup of vinegar added to the rinse cycle works as a laundry softener.

COOKIES

Cookies were as much part of our tuck boxes as the candies.

Canadian Cookies	34
Chocolate Crunchies	35
Chocolate Grathams	36
Langues-de-chat	37
Melting Moments	38
Nig Nags	39
Pinwheels	40
Shortbread	41

Cookies were the last thing our camp cook, Debbie, made for us in the Arctic. While she was taking a batch from the oven, a curious lemming fell onto the grate above the grill, scaring the bejasus out of her. Our Inuit motor man, Simeon, came to her rescue. He extracted the terrified lemming from above the grate; flipped out his clasp knife, slit open the rodent's belly and scarfed it down, bones, guts and all. Finally, Simeon dropped the pelt neatly into the garbage bucket, wiped his mouth on a napkin: then, smiling at Debbie, belched politely behind his hand as he strolled back to work. Turned green, retching, she disappeared from the kitchen. She only emerged two days later, when she left on the next plane out, never to return.

Heinlein's advice on cats.

Never try to outstubborn a cat.
(this also applies to dachshunds)

He extracted the terrified lemming from the grate, flipped out his clasp knife, slit open the rodent's belly and scarfed it down, bones, guts and all.

Canadian Cookies

I remember, as a very small child (probably only 5 years of age), a roll of these cookies being sliced in the kitchen of great uncle Wullie's ranch Driefontein; which our Scots family called Three Fountains, and the ranch hands called Umanzimtatu; but I cannot remember who was making them, only a big bum in her navy blue polka dotted skirt! Even today, about seventy years later, the delicious smell of these cookies, fresh out the oven, evokes memories of that skirt.

Requirements:

8 oz unsalted butter	3 eggs
1 tsp bicarbonate of soda	2 tsp vanilla essence
1 cup minced nuts	1 cup sugar
4 oz bitter chocolate	4 cups flour
1 tsp baking powder	pinch of salt

Instructions:

Cream butter and sugar, then add vanilla and the eggs one at a time, beating constantly. Sift together the flour, salt, bicarbonate of soda and baking powder, adding slowly to mixture while continuing to beat. Finally break the chocolate into pea sized chips and add with the chopped nuts, then roll dough into 12 inch cylinders 2 inches in diameter on floured board. Wrap each roll in waxed paper and chill overnight.

Cut roll into thin slices, lay on greased and floured baking tray and bake at 400°F for 12-15 mins until light brown. Makes a large quantity and keeps well in an airtight tin.

This recipe comes from my great grandmother, who certainly never set foot on Canadian soil; so whence comes the name, I know not! My guess is that the crude chocolate chips speak to its distant origins.

Pinot Noir

I sent our *'presque-fille'*, Marie-Claude, a bottle of Pinot Noir for her birthday. A week later I received her prognosis: "Shoot the horse!"

Chocolate Crunchies

Cousin Gaynor, eldest daughter of my father's "baby" brother, John, contributed this take on ANZAC cookies. For her, everything good was always "just divine"; while anything bad was almost certain to give her mother "conniptions", if she heard about it. Any slip, and her mother would "have a cat". As is obvious from the recipe, she admires simplicity.

Requirements:

    1 cup each flour, coconut, oatmeal.

    $^1/_2$ cup brown sugar

    6 oz butter

    1 tsp baking powder

Instructions:

Mix the dry ingredients, add melted butter. Knead. Place on greased baking tray. Bake at 300°F for 30 minutes.

    Topping: *(for variety, not compulsory)*

      2 cups frosting sugar   1 tblsp cocoa

      Mix together with a little hot water.

Uncle John was 12 years my father's junior. Their mother died in the Spanish 'flu when he was an infant, so my father was virtual mother to the youngest boys until my grandfather remarried. John used to complain, even when he was over sixty, that my father still treated him like a child!

John, who was deafened at El Alamein when his artillery piece exploded, wore a hearing aid in one shirt pocket, and a transistor radio in the other. He'd switch to the latter to keep up to date on cricket scores.

When I met Gaynor's granddaughters for the first time, I sported a moustache; on the basis that if you have something outstanding, underline it. They stared at me before running to fetch their great grandfather's photograph. He and I were identical, moustache and all!

Goo Remover

Use eucalyptus oil to remove the latex goo from your skin after using a band-aid. WD40 works even better.

Chocolate Grathams

I have no idea what a gratham is: perhaps a Scots or Gaelic word, or maybe called after someone of that name. They are good, but if you foul up, they will be as hard as hockey pucks. When that happened, for good reason our foster sisters called them "Dentist Biscuits".

Requirements:

2 cups flour	1 cup berry sugar
1 tsp bicarbonate of soda	1 egg
4 oz unsalted butter	$^1/_3$ cup cocoa powder
Pinch of salt	

Instructions:

Cream together butter and half sugar, then beat in remaining sugar and beaten egg. Sift together flour, cocoa, salt and soda, add slowly to creamed ingredients, and work quickly to smooth stiff dough. Break off walnut sized pieces and roll into little balls. Put balls about 2 inches apart on greased baking tray. Bake in very slow oven (250°F) until firm to touch.

This takes at least 20 mins, but a lot depends on altitude, barometric pressure and humidity: hence the dentist moniker.

As you take them from oven, sprinkle with a little berry sugar to give extra oomph to their appearance. Store in an airtight tin.

Apart from the taste, the neatest thing about these cookies is the cracks across their tops. When my grandmother made one of her rare "hockey puck" batches, my brother and I earned a well deserved tongue and bum lashing on a picnic, when we used them as skipping stones on the Reservoir lake. Our "angelic" foster sisters, who started the idea, escaped her wrath by pleading innocence by virtue of gender.

Fluffy Whipped Cream

Add the white of an egg to cream before whipping. The cream will be stiffer, fluffier, and will go twice as far; but this tip might kill you, the egg white being uncooked.

Langues-de-chat

These are the quintessential French cookie, usually served with fruit salad, or other light dessert. They are surprisingly simple to make, but carry all the dignity and sophistication of haute-cuisine!

The name "cats' tongues" tells it all. These are wonderfully delicate.

Requirements:

$^1/_2$ cup flour	$^1/_2$ cup berry sugar
2 oz salted softened butter	1 egg.

1 tsp pure vanilla extract (real stuff, not artificial garbage)

Instructions:

Cream butter and sugar, then add vanilla and egg. Beat vigorously and thoroughly until smooth. Using sieve, slowly mix in flour by hand. Transfer batter to Ziplock bag, clip quarter inch hole off one corner, and use to squeeze 2 inch long sausages onto lightly oiled papered baking tray. Each sausage should be 1 inch from others, as they spread as they cook. Bake 5 mins in preheated oven at 350°F until golden. Do not overcook. Remove from oven and allow to cool on the baking tray.

Best eaten freshly baked, but they can keep relatively fresh in an airtight tin for a few days.

Beware! You cannot sample just one, and putting them out to cool is an open invitation to larceny for kids and spouse. One such incident, which occurred over thirty years ago, just prior to a dinner party, was regarded as grounds for divorce, despite the clear provocation and temptation. It cost me pearl earrings to rectify the "misunderstanding"; but there still remains a festering wound of resentment at the theft.

In retrospect, was it worth it?

Try them yourself, and you answer!

Household Hint

Put an old nylon stocking over a yardstick, splash on some vinegar and clear the dust bunnies from beneath fridge or stove.

Melting Moments

These are particularly well named, they're really delicious, and were one of my mother's specialties. There are 2 quite different recipes that mother used, both listed under the same name. She saw no paradox in this, as my father, who would not eat custard under any circumstances (unless he was ignorant of its presence), was not allowed to know the ingredients of type 'B', his favourite cookie.

Requirements:

Type 'A'	Type 'B'
$^3/_4$ cup flour	1 cup flour
$^1/_4$ cup corn flour	$^1/_2$ cup custard powder
pinch salt	pinch salt
1 tsp vanilla essence	1 tsp vanilla essence
$^1/_2$ cup frosting sugar	$^1/_2$ cup castor sugar
4 oz butter	4 oz butter

Instructions:

Sift together flour, corn flour/ custard powder and salt in one bowl. Cream butter, vanilla and sugar in another, then work in dry ingredients using back of wooden spoon. Roll into walnut-sized balls, or smaller, place on greased pan and flatten with back of fork. Decorate with a glacé cherry; or if you're parsimonious like mother, use only half cherry. Instead, use chocolate chip or angelica. Bake at 375°F for 10-15 mins, until pale buff. If desired, sprinkle with coloured sprinkles, coloured berry sugar, or coarse coffee sugar. When cold, join with lemon butter icing, or not.

Like langues-de-chat, *these are irresistible, but so far are innocent of being the cause of any marital disharmony in our family.*

Fresh Eggs

Fresh eggs sink; rotten eggs float. As an egg ages, the blunt end fills with a mixture of methane, carbon dioxide and hydrogen sulphide, causing that end to rise when put in water.

Nig-Nags

These come from my great grandfather William, a master baker (that's baker, you, with the mind like a sewer) and confectioner by trade, who ran the bakery attached to great grandmother Café. She was a tyrannical matriarch, but a cannie businesswoman: he was a drunk, but a brilliant baker. In partnership with his son "big" Archie, great grandfather owned a successful racehorse, for which they stole eggs from the bakery to condition it for race days at the Turf Club. Our Kiwi neighbour bakes an identical cookie, which she and our Aussie cousins call Anzac biscuits.

Requirements:

    1 cup each desiccated grated coconut, rolled oats, Demerara sugar, flour

    1 tblsp golden syrup   4 oz butter

    1 tblsp bicarbonate of soda   2 tblsp cold water

Instructions:

Mix dry ingredients in large bowl. Melt butter in small pan; add syrup, then bicarbonate of soda. Stir into dry ingredients, rinse pan with the cold water and add to mixture, mix well. Put walnut sized lumps 1 inch apart on buttered baking tray. Bake 45 minutes in moderate oven (275°F) until flat and brown. Cool on tray. Store in airtight tin, well out of reach of, and hidden from, children, grandchildren and spouses. They never last long.

Big" Archie's son, "wee" Archie, rose through the ranks to become a full general, known to his troops as "Red-'n-'orrible", during the civil war. "Big" Archie had an elder brother, "wee" Wullie, aka William to a Sassenach, a recluse who was not a full box of chocolates. He must have been nuts, for he hated baking: hated the feel of flour on his hands.

To Preserve Eggs

Boil together $2^1/_2$ quarts of water with 1 lb slaked lime and 2 lb salt. Cool. Meanwhile wash 2 dozen very fresh raw eggs. Immerse the eggs in the solution for 20 minutes. They'll stay fresh for at least 6 months *(or so my grandmother says!)*.

Pinwheels

Another favourite of my mother, but only made when she was making meringues, so as not to waste the egg whites!

Requirements:

4 oz butter	$^2/_3$ cup sugar
1 egg yolk	3-4 tblsp whole milk
2 tblsp cocoa powder	2 cups flour
2 tsp baking powder	1 tsp vanilla essence
pinch salt	

Instructions:

In a teacup, blend cocoa to thick paste with few drops hot water. In large bowl, cream butter, yolk, sugar and vanilla and beat. Sift in all dry ingredients, alternating with milk, to form thick dough. Split dough into equal halves and knead cocoa paste into one half. Roll out both doughs onto waxed paper sheets, then place brown on white. After removing waxed paper (!) roll them together into a tight cylinder, about 2 inch diameter. Wrap in wax paper, chill until very hard, then slice to $^1/_4$ inch thickness and bake on a buttered tray at 375°F for 10 minutes.

Alternative to pinwheel is to have a third layer, with or without cocoa colouring. Lay out the double layer, slice it in two and lay the one half upon other, slice longitudinally again, then flip one half to lie beside other. Lay the multicoloured and reconstituted dough on third layer and wrap into cylinder. Once chilled and cut, you'll have checkerboard cookies.

As a child I consistently whipped my grandfather's friend Ludovick at chess: so he quit the game, giving me his century old chess set, which I've since given to my son, who consistently whips me.

Brown Floor Polish

Chop up 3 wax candles and a bar of laundry soap really finely and melt on the stove, stirring in a small tin of boot polish, a cup of turpentine and $1^1/_2$ cups kerosene. Allow to set for 2 days.

Shortbread

Whenever we went to visit Aunt Bella (my mother's great aunt, who lived in perfect health and lucidity until age 96), we were served tea and shortbread. Her friend, Aunt Maud, who was the great aunt of my sister-in-law, sniffed at her, as a "mere pup". Maud lived to age 103, also lucid and healthy to the end.

Bella never had a bad word for anyone. Her fiancé was killed in the Great War, so she remained unmarried all her life. When well into her eighties, she declined to try on a medieval chastity belt, which found its way to the farm, because she said it was about sixty years too late...

"...I might be on the shelf, but I've been down to be dusted a time or two!" she explained in her soft highland lilt.

<u>Requirements</u>

1 cup flour	1 cup corn flour
1 cup berry sugar	1 cup soft unsalted butter
1 cup more flour!	pinch of salt

<u>Instructions:</u>

Sift together dry ingredients, mix them, then sift together once more. Rub in butter, until it's a smooth stiff dough. Lightly butter wax-papered baking tray. Press dough into baking tray to an even thickness of about an inch. Prick all over. Bake at 300°F for 20 mins. Remove from oven, cut into 3 x 1 inch fingers, without separating shapes. Return to oven and bake for a further 30 to 40 mins until just pale buff. Sprinkle with berry sugar, turn off oven and leave inside oven until cool.

Shortbread is the only baking that tastes almost as good when it's stale! It always goes down remarkably well with good champagne: but then, everything goes down remarkably well with good champagne (and with poor champagne, too, come to think of it!).

Au Gratin

A dish sprinkled with breadcrumbs and butter, then browned under the grill. Originally, it had nothing to do with cheese.

JAMS, JELLIES & PRESERVES

Knowing how much I enjoy hot, English-style mustard when she served gammon steaks or roast beef, Debbie, the camp cook, made up a jar of "the good stuff", with oil and vinegar, suitably fortified with fresh horseradish to give it that extra little "oomph". Hungry, after a hard twelve-hour shift, extending the runway on the esker beside the camp, Simeon, her Inuit nemesis, was first in line for a mountain of roast beef, potatoes and "yorkies", all half drowned in rich brown gravy. He plonked himself beside me, lathering the gaps on his plate with any preserves within his ample reach, including a generous dollop of my "special" mustard, which he had never tasted before. With an air of contentment, he began to shovel the food down his gullet.

Suddenly, Simeon froze. He sighed, exhaling heavily through his nose. Tears sprang unbidden to his eyes, trickling down his cheeks as he fought to swallow. I could almost hear his sinuses clearing as the fiery fumes flushed his nasal passages. As finally he swallowed, he managed a weak smile, then he nodded to me.

"Good!" he croaked, as he dumped another tablespoonful of the mustard concoction on his plate. "Yes, good!"

Hospitality

True hospitality is making your guests feel like they *are* at home...

...all the while you really wish they *were* at home!

Marula Jelly

Although these are probably the most abundant wild fruit in subtropical southern Africa, there's a dearth of them in north America: no problem, substitute crab apples for the marulas (also spelt maroelas, but more correctly amarula, *or in western Zimbabwe* m'kanu *(not to be confused with* mqanu, *which is a type of wood, from the* mqhanu *tree, or* m'ganu *which is a plate)*)*

To collect fruit, sweep up all old marulas from under tree and discard. Come back next day and collect fruit, which will be mostly still very green (which is good, as it sets better, for some goofy reason) from under tree. Wash fruit, then with a sharp knife, circle them. Toss about 10lbs of fruit in a pot, just cover with water, and boil for about half an hour. Strain and squeeze, toss fruit, and retain fluid, which is now murky yellow-grey sludge. For every quart of fluid, add juice of a lemon (or better yet, lime), a scraping of zest, and 2 lb of sugar. Warm fluid gently to dissolve sugar, turn up heat and boil the heck out of it for half an hour, by which time it should be either orange or pink. Bottle and cool.

> **The **mq** click is made by slamming the tongue from the roof down to the floor of the mouth, quite distinct from **xh** which comes from the cheeks, and from **nc** achieved by slipping the tongue down from the upper front teeth. Included in the click repertoire is **dhl** which sounds like a drunk who wants to sdlheep it off; and **qh** which sounds like you're trying to suck a booger back from your nasal passages.*

So now you know how to make marula jelly: all you need to find is a marula tree out on the prairies

With a bit of practice, you should also be able to click like a Xhosa!

Bain Marie

A large shallow pan of hot water, big enough to hold several pots. Used for keeping sauces warm, or for gentle cooking, like custards.

Preserved Mangoes

Mango season played havoc with our guts. The fruit was plentiful, the trees grew everywhere, the cost was nil. They came in an infinite spectrum of different varieties: little 'peach' mangoes, red and orange; giant oumas *that were always slightly green, even when ripe; kidney mangoes, as big as calf kidneys; yellow sabres, sweet, Oh, so sweet. Mango season brought a flurry of activity in the kitchen, making chutney, jam and mango preserve.*

Requirements:

Use green mangoes.
equal weight of sugar
equal weight of water (1lb = 1 pint)
1tsp grated fresh ginger per 2 lb fruit
zest and juice of 1 lime per 2lb fruit

Instructions:

Peel and pit the mangoes. Weigh the fruit.

Stirring slowly, bring the water and sugar to the boil, ensuring that all sugar is dissolved. Drop in fruit, ginger and lime zest and juice: boil until tender and translucent. Bottle and seal.

As infants, we were never allowed by my grandmother to eat mangoes anywhere but naked in the bath. It made it a lot easier to clean us up afterwards! We did the same to our children.

When my prissy godmother arrived fresh from Europe in mango season, my grandfather, her uncle, could not restrain himself, and rubbed her face with a mango pit "to lighten her up". It didn't work: she was always toffee-nosed and priggish.

Grandfather and his daughter (my mother) had another irritating habit. In grape season they shot the seeds around the dining room. My daughter, my son and I never would do such a thing: we shoot cherry pits, but grapes were banned when mum visited.

Mango Fool

Peel 4 very ripe mangoes. Rub through sieve, or rip in blender until it's paste. Whip 1 cup cream, fold into mangoes. Serve immediately.

...we were never allowed by my grandmother
to eat mangos anywhere but naked in the bath.

Green Mango Chutney

Everyone has his own recipe: a recipe better that that of anyone else. If you must buy, rather than make chutney; look for the "Major Grey" style, which is exactly how chutney should be.

Requirements:

1$^1/_2$ lb green mango meat	$^3/_4$ lb raisins
$^3/_4$ lb sultanas	1$^1/_2$ lb apples
1lb Demerara sugar	2 pints vinegar
2 tsp salt	12 cloves
2 jalapeños	

Instructions:

Dice the fruit, put in a pot at very low heat and simmer in its own juices for 30 minutes. Then heat up vinegar and sugar in separate pot to dissolve sugar, add spices, and add to the fruit. Cover and simmer for an hour or more. Pour to just overflowing while hot into warm jars, cover and seal while hot.

The Khmer, with whom I worked for six years, prefer mangoes raw and green, rather than ripe or cooked in any way. They peel and slice the mango, then dip in a mixture of sugar, salt and cayenne pepper. It is tasty, but too much raw mango exacts a vicious toll of Sihanouk's Revenge, with serious after burn, similar to Mexican heartburn.

Mangoes are not the only fruit the Khmer prefer green. They pick their oranges way too soon, and tomatoes always seem too green. They even have a delicious banana, the skin of which never turns yellow, but remains forever green.

The language barrier breeds its own problems. When I ordered a beer in Siem Reap, it came without the customary salted peanuts, so I called the waiter back, demanding some snacks. He listened intently, then disappeared. Ten minutes later I was served a grilled snake.

Vol-Au-Vent

Before putting *vol-au-vent* cases in the oven, prick them four times at equal intervals with a skewer. This ensures the sides rise evenly.

"If you worry, you die: if you don't worry, you still die. So why worry?" Alfred
E. Newman

Tomato and Apricot Chutney

Mangoes are not the only fruit from which chutney can be made; I think my mother tried just about every fruit in our extensive orchard on the farm, not least being windfall apples, green peaches, guavas and papayas. She even tried turnips, which was not a bad experiment. For north Americans, here's a less exotic recipe:

Requirements:

    1lb dried apricots, or 2lb unripe apricots

2lb greener tomatoes	1 large onion
1 lb brown sugar	1 tsp salt
4 cloves	6 allspice berries
1 tsp cayenne pepper	1 cup vinegar

Instructions:

If using dried apricots, soak them overnight. Otherwise, stone the apricots, dice them, onion and tomatoes and simmer until soft, add the vinegar, sugar and spices and simmer for a couple of hours. Pour piping hot into warmed jars until slightly overflowing, cover and seal while hot.

Chutney is not only for curry. It is excellent on roast beef sandwiches; about forty years ago, my then pregnant spouse ate a full jar with a half pound of cheddar in one sitting, suffering no ill effects. And our son, the result of that pregnancy, seems relatively normal.

A spoonful of chutney in vinaigrette really kicks that up a notch; a spoonful in guacamole is a life changing experience.

Tastes in chutney vary. I like mine chunky; others prefer it as a sludge. I'm a fan of sweet chutney, to counter a spicy curry: others like theirs fiery. Some like it sloppy, like a sauce: my preference is firm.

Maître d'Hôtel Butter

Knead 4 oz butter until soft. Mix thoroughly with 1 tblsp parsley, $1/_2$ tsp salt, good pinch of coarse ground pepper, juice of $1/_4$ lemon, and 1 tblsp mustard powder if desired.

Achar or Atjar

As Catsup is to Canada, so Achar is to southern Africa; the essential condiment on every table. Originating in India, the name merely means delicious in Hindi. Enjoy it on cold chicken and on ham or cheese sandwiches. Our kids were fed it in liberal quantities in school lunches. Nephew Hilton treats achar as an indispensable food group, eating it as an accompaniment to everything, even on its own.

Requirements:

1 cucumber	1 carrot
1 cup butter beans	1 cup green beans
1 egg fruit	1 green pepper
1 corgette (aka zuccini)	1 onion
juice & zest of 1 lime	5 almonds
1 tsp tumeric	1 inch ginger root
4 cloves garlic and then some	2 cups vinegar
2 tsp Demerara sugar	olive oil
10 green peppercorns	

Instructions:

Slice the vegetables into thin sticks; boil in minimum chicken stock for 5 minutes. Pound almonds, tumeric, peppercorns, ginger, garlic, zest & lime juice to a paste. Mix with vinegar, add to vegetables and season with salt & sugar to taste. Simmer for 5 minutes. Pour hot into warmed wide mouthed jars, top up with olive oil.

Like much of Natal-kwaZulu cuisine, achar came to the country with the East Indians, who were brought in as indentured labour for the sugar estates. South Africa now has the largest ethnic Indian population in the world, outside of India.

Al Dente

Cooked until it offers the slightest resistance to the teeth. With the exception of green *mielies* (sweet corn), squashes, artichokes and potatoes, this is how all vegetables should be.

Pepper Relish

*This is a good recipe to use when preparing brown bag lunches. Like achar
and chutney, this does make life a little different when put on roast beef, ham or
cheese sandwiches.*

Requirements:

12 sweet green peppers	3 large onions
12 sweet red peppers	4 cups vinegar
12 yellow banana peppers	2 cups brown sugar
4 tsp salt	12 cloves garlic
2 tblsp fresh thyme leaves	

Instructions:

Split peppers and remove seeds, then chop coarsely, cover with boiling
water, stand for 5 mins; drain and repeat, and repeat, drain and dry on paper.
Chop onions coarsely and slice garlic thinly; mix with peppers and thyme.
Boil together sugar, salt and vinegar until dissolved, add other ingredients and
boil 10 mins. Pack while hot into hot jars until overflowing, seal while hot.

*My brother fancied himself a falconer. His first try, a fledgling bought off a
peasant, turned out to be a vulture, that could poep through the eye of a needle at
15 paces. He sold the problem to another sucker.*

*Next were two eagle owls, named Pawpaw (that's what Australians and
South Africans call a papaya) and Mango. Once they could fly, they ate our father's
pigeons, compounding the felony by taking up residence in the empty dovecote.*

*Mother took a hand, feeding each bird every evening with a dead mouse
zapped earlier by her ratting terrier; calling them: "Paw-paw, Mango!" until they
took the offering from her hand.*

Sandwiches

To make sandwiches, use only bread that is 24hours old: fresh bread does not cut
so cleanly.

> **"The light at the end of the tunnel just might be a train coming the other way."**
> **Anon**

Mustard Pickles

This is an attempted copy of the great British pickle called Chow-chow or Piccalilli. Perhaps it's not quite there, but it is delicious. When I was working in the Zambezi valley in the late 60s, I enjoyed this pickle with game meat, particularly young warthog, which is probably the best meat in the African bush.

Requirements:

2 pints vinegar	1 cup sugar
1 tblsp tumeric	1 tblsp mustard
2 tblsp corn flour	

1 gallon of vegetables: cauliflower, carrots, corn off the cob, cucumber, courgette (aka zucchini)

Instructions:

Cut up vegetables to thumbnail size. Parboil the carrots, corn, cauliflower. Soak all overnight in salty water. Meanwhile mix together dry ingredients with a little vinegar to form a paste, then stir the paste gradually into boiling vinegar, and boil until thick. Stir in the vegetables, heat them through but do not boil. Pour hot into prewarmed jars to overflowing and seal while hot.

A game ranger neighbour in the Zambezi valley raised Geraldine, an orphan warthog; which, after being suckled by his Ridgeback-Stafford cross, identified with her pups as a dog. Geraldine was perfectly house trained from an early age; and, apart from rooting in the vegetable patch, her sole vice was chasing cars with the other dogs. This was the inevitable cause of her early demise, when she was run over. Geraldine's foster mother met a similar fate when they moved to town, and she attacked the rear wheel of a garbage truck.

Bouquet Garni

A bunch of herbs, tied together or in a muslin baggie, used for flavouring sauces soups or casseroles. Most commonly consists of thyme, bay leaf, parsley, occasionally celery, marjoram and others.

her sole vice was chasing cars with the other dogs...

Pickled Cauliflower

I've no idea where this is from, as I don't recognize the spidery writing. However, I remember this, or a variant of this, in our tuck boxes when we were at high school. It is pretty good with cold roast beef.

Requirements:

Cauliflowers	salt
water	peppercorns
allspice berries	piripiri chillies
vinegar	brown sugar

How much of everything? Just kinda guess it!!!!

Instructions:

Break up and boil cauliflower for 5 mins in brine, Drain and pack into jars. Estimate how much vinegar you'll need to fill the voids, and then some, put that amount in a pot, add sugar, piripiri, pepper and allspice berries to taste, and bring to boil. Strain the vinegar, splitting the non-liquid equally between jars of cauliflower, then fill jars to brim with hot vinegar. Seal while hot.

Great uncle George, Bella's kid brother, was a huge pickle fan. When he and my father worked together for some years, they shared their brown-bag lunches, but never his pickles. George refused to work afternoons, because it interfered with his fishing; which he did every day, rain or shine, in or out of season. He told us that, as a child, the family had moved from the Highlands to the banks of the Clyde, into which the family biffy discharged.

"Aye, an' we cacht mony a braw fish an' a' in the Clyde, richt by the hoos."

"You didn't eat them?" asked my father, who had a queasy stomach

"Och, aye!" George replied, "'twere the only time we'd ever got oor own back, so to speak, d'ye ken?"

Back Seat Drivers

Some women do drive from the back seat, just like their husbands who cook from the dining room.

Pickled Onions

Lunch for me is generally just fresh bread with cheese and pickles, perhaps cold meat, radishes, celery and green onions. But lunch isn't real if there's no pickled onion with the cheese.

Requirements:

at least 1 lb of pearl onions	mace
a dozen garlic cloves	peppercorns
small Thai chillies (one per Mason Jar)	
allspice berries	

Instructions:

Peel onions; soak 24 hours in strong brine. Drain, boil in fresh solution of brine for 5 mins. Drain, soak 6 hours in cold water. Put selection of chillies, garlic, pepper and allspice corns and mace into each jar, then pack jars with onions and heat in bain marie. Boil enough vinegar and then some, to just cover the onions, and pour over onions while hot. Seal immediately.

During a stint in the army, when I was in a maShona *militia unit guarding a local village, the fatigues detail were digging up and eating what looked like pearl onions. I traded a pile of them for a 6-pack, then pickled them. But they were a grass corm, which tasted foul when pickled!*

In the same village, Sergeant Swando put a detail to collecting wild aloes to beautify the village. As they seemed reluctant to handle the plants, I showed the men how to strip the dead leaves. I was immediately zapped by a scorpion lurking in the roots. The pain was instantaneous and extraordinary, like a white-hot wire wriggling in my hand, which swelled to twice its size. I was helped to my hut by Swando, remembering little of the next two days, until I awoke in hospital, with a doctor beside me.

"Did you think you were dying?" he asked.

I nodded, weakly.

"So did I!" he replied, as he left my side.

Fish Marinade

Never marinade fish for over an hour: it absorbs flavour very quickly.

Pickled Gherkins

Wherever you come from, a gherkin is the quintessential pickle. You really cannot eat hamburgers without a gherkin, a slice of raw onion and a slice of tomato. A BLT is not a BLT without as slice of gherkin; cold chicken has nothing, without the oomph that a gherkin imparts.

Requirements:

2 gallons small pickling gherkins	salt aplenty
4 cups vinegar	1 cup water
2 tsp mustard seeds	abundant fresh dill
1 tblsp dill seed	12 garlic cloves

Instructions:

Soak gherkins overnight in medium brine solution, drain, rinse, and add to pot of boiling vinegar, water, herbs and spices, turn down heat for 5 minutes then remove, strain off, retaining both solids and liquids. Pack gherkins with herbs and spices into warmed jars, pour in hot solution to overflowing, being careful to tap out any air bubbles. Seal while hot.

The guard dog on the gold mining camp at Guanay, in the yambas of Bolivia, would do anything for a pickled gherkin. While his partner, Boris, on the other fence could not even be bribed with a fresh sirloin steak, young César would sidle up to anyone and mooch if he could smell dill pickles.

Sokha, the cook at our exploration camp in Cambodia kept a couple of geese, as alarm guards and to keep the snakes down. One goose took a fancy to me, after I fed her a cucumber, and thereafter gave me no peace unless I gave her another. I still have bruises from where she (the goose, not Sokha) bit my thigh to get my attention.

Ginger

Never grate ginger, except in the smallest amounts. Scrape or peel it, then slice and chop it. 2 tblsp of fresh chopped ginger is about equivalent to $1/_2$ tsp of ground dry ginger.

One goose took a fancy to me after I fed her a cucumber,
and there after gave me no peace unless I gave her another.

"Get your facts first... then you can distort them as much as you please." Mark Twain

---

Lemon Curd

As far back as I can remember, there was lemon curd on the farm. Being in the tropics, there were lemon trees everywhere; being a poultry farm, there was no shortage of raw material.

My brother, our foster sisters and I were given jars of it in our school tuck boxes; and when there were no cookies for us, my grandmother fed us bread slathered with lemon curd. It went into tarts; onto scones and pancakes and was always our favourite filling in a sandwich cake

Requirements:

2 cups sugar	4 oz butter
6 eggs	juice of 4-6 lemons
zest of 1-2 lemons	

Instructions:

Melt together sugar, juice. zest and butter. Beat the eggs enthusiastically, then add to the pot, constantly stirring. Continue stirring and transfer pot to a double boiler. Cook until thick, stirring constantly. Pour hot into warmed jars and seal immediately.

My great aunt Nell, grandmother's kid sister, was a lemon curd aficionada, making lime curd, tangelo curd and lemon-lime curd as well as the regular variety. Hers was a tragic life, for her first and only child was killed by a drive-by motor accident before his teens. Like her young aunt Bella, she lost her fiancé in the Great War, and both her first and second husbands died young.

For some reason, Aunt Nell took a great fancy to me, leaving me everything she owned in her will, except her condo, which I was to share with my brother and 11 cousins! We sold it.

Bacon

Always cook more bacon than necessary, and make sure it's crispy and oil free. Crush it up and freeze it. Then use as an unusual topping and seasoning for soups, salads and stews.

I ordered the frog soup, recommended by Guillermo, in Tilcomayo, between Lima to La Oraya. The soup smelt delicious, but no matter how I turned the plate, the frog, fixed with a toothpick to a potato, kept staring at me. I traded plates with Chico, the Mine manager, who had ordered roast guinea pig. It was just as appetizing, but didn't watch me.

SOUPS

I overheard my American client scolding his Mongolian mistress for an extravagant shopping spree, to which she responded:

"For me you buy the beautiful horse boots for to wear. Also I ride horse. I eat horse in the soup I cooks. I drinks milk from horse in airag *and* arkhi. *Now, what? You wants I must dress also like the horse? No! You can to find another one girlfriend, she who looks like the horse. Me? I go. I find another one boyfriend."*

I was assured by another colleague, who overheard the same exchange, that her extravagance was a regular complaint of our client; and the response was almost identical at every change of season, when the fashion conscious lady splashed out on her new wardrobe.

> "Happiness is when what you think, what you say, and what you do are in harmony." Mohandas Gandhi

Princess Tecuichpoch Soup

I was introduced to this in Morelia, capital of Michoacán by my mining partner José. It is named for the daughter of Moctezuma, Tecuichpoch Ixcaxochitzin (really, that was her name!), who was widowed 5 times, bore Cortes an illegitimate daughter, and later married a Spaniard, and died in Spain. I was surprised to find avocado in a hot dish, and more surprised by the exceptional blend of flavours.

<u>Requirements</u>

2 tortillas (corn)	splash olive oil
1 onion	8 cloves garlic
2 jalapeno peppers	2 banana peppers
$1/_2$ lb chicken breasts	4 cups chicken bouillon
Juice of 5 limes	zest of 1 lime
2 tomatoes	salt to taste
1 tsp peppercorns	1 avocado
1 handful cilantro	

<u>Instructions:</u>

Thinly slice onion, garlic and peppers; fry in soup pot until onions are translucent and lightly caramelized. Slice chicken breasts very thin, roll in lime zest and peppercorns, add to pot, toss briefly, then douse with chicken bouillon and lime juice, salt to taste. Peel and seed tomatoes, then add. Simmer 10 mins. Meanwhile slice tortillas to $1/_2$ inch strips, bake 5 mins at 400°F until light brown and crispy, then keep warm in basket. Chop cilantro very fine, dice avocado, add both to soup; bring back to boil. Serve immediately, with crispy communal tortilla strips to add individually.

When In Doubt, Use Vinegar

Use vinegar to clean everything from garbage cans to shower curtains.

Sea Critter Chowder

Here is absolute simplicity, and a delicious healthy pick-me-up on a dreary winter night. Invite a couple of friends around to help enjoy it, if they can bring the wine: but make sure you tell them to bring an expensive bottle! We usually shuck a few raw PEI oysters as an aperitif.

When shucking oysters, always use a thick leather glove, or have your son-in-law do the shucking. That way you won't injure yourself.

Requirements:

1 spud per person, plus 1	1 sweet red pepper
2 sticks celery	1 onion
1 small carrot per person	1 beer
1 bottle clam juice	1 can baby clams
1 can tuna flakes	chicken-in-a-bottle
2 clams per person	2 mussels per person
2 shrimps per person	3 shakes Tabasco
1-2 cups mashed potatoes	1 cup frozen peas
1 tsp peppercorns	1 tsp allspice berries
1 lb frozen mixed fruits-de-mer	
(scallops, mini squid, clams, scampi)	

Instructions:

With the exception of seafood, mashed potatoes and peas, dice everything really fine, cover with beer, add squirt of chicken-in-a-bottle, and boil gently until carrots are done, say 25 mins. Thaw and drain frozen critters. Break tuna into broth and stir in, then mix mashed potato and clam juice to a thick slurry and add to broth. Finally add seafood and peas, and simmer for 5 mins, or until prawns are pink.

Served with fresh bread, and washed down with beer, this will remind you how things ought to be all the time. Keep the wine that the guests brought to enjoy on your own: if they wanted wine with the meal they should have brought 4 bottles.

Stamp Out Organized Crime: Ban the IRS.

Turkey Balls Soup

Originating in one of those snob gourmet magazines that insists on complicating everything, this underwent a major revamp, replacing gnocchi with diced potatoes; plain simple salt, instead of that pink Himalayan garbage (the pink is from dirt and critters trapped in the crystal lattice), and so forth. The result is infinitely better than the original, became standard winter lunch fare, when this soup improves by the day.

Requirements:

Broth	Turkey balls
8 cups chicken stock	1 lb ground turkey
1 cup of each	2 tblsp grated cheese
carrots, potatoes	1 tblsp mustard
onion, leek, celery	2 tblsp corn flake crumbs
tomato frozen peas	2 tblsp olive oil
salt, pepper, thyme, parsley, green onions	

Instructions:

Broth Layer chopped vegetables in bottom of soup pot with a splash of oil and cook, stirring occasionally until onions are transparent. Add stock.

Turkey balls Meanwhile, mix turkey with a little oil, the mustard, cheese and crumbs, roll into walnut sized balls and drop into broth. Stir gently then simmer until meatballs are cooked. Add peas about 10 mins before serving. Add chopped parsley and chopped green onions to each bowl as you serve.

In Cambodia a similar soup is breakfast: for potatoes, use noodles; for turkey, chicken; instead of ground meat, chop a bird up, bones and all, into unmanageably small pieces. We called it grenade chicken soup. The squiggly bits (heart, liver, gizzard and other unmentionables) were cooked with the rest. If Sokha, the camp cook, really likes you, you get extra squiggly bits. She is the Khmer incarnation of Debbie, the arctic wonder.

If you're a Philistine and use canned instead of fresh asparagus, open the can on the bottom, to prevent damaging the tips.

"If you're too stupid to make soup, there's no help for you." Me

---

Musgo Soup

The Railway Cafe in Carrievale, southeast Saskatchewan, had musgo lunch special once a month for $4.²². Whatever was in the fridge, nearing its best-before date was a "Must Go". One guy got gammon steak; the next, a burger, or pickerel fillet, or pork cutlet!

Requirements:

Open ye icebox: what seest thou?

If it moveth, kill it and toss it out; if it moveth not, yet hath hair, toss it out; if it moveth not, and 'tis on the savoury side of edible, use it: if unsavoury, toss it: if on the sweet side, let it be.

Half a sausage? Lonely hamburger? Perfect, chop 'em up. Spaghetti sauce? Left over chilli? Chicken leg? Mac and cheese? Why not? Bowl of cold mashed potatoes? Certainly, but keep it as thickening. Cabbage? Tomatoes? Spinach? Sure, no problem, depending on your taste. Four beers? Of course! Pull 'em and put to one side.

Iceberg lettuce... Iceberg lettuce?! *Are you off your perch?* That's not food, that's what food eats.

Left-over pizza? Nah, keep it for breakfast.

Instructions:

Put all in ye pot, add one beer. Turn heat to minimum, add some water if necessary. Then relax with the other beer, its brother, and another. After half an hour ye soup be done. Grind in ye blender, add mashed potato, season to taste *et voila*! Musgo *soupe du jour*.

The Carrievale Cafe had another idiosyncrasy: their water was so brackish that it was acceptable for customers to bring their own coffee with them, provided they shared with other patrons and the owners.

Meat Marinade

An aromatic bath of wine, spices, herbs and vegetables for uncooked meat. The object, apart from imparting a special flavour, is either to tenderize tough cuts, or to moisten dry meat like venison or rabbit.

Marrowbone Consommé

For a bubleaas regmaker *(hangover cure) there's nothing quite like bone marrow on toast. It is rich, full of cholesterol, greasy and pure poison for your arteries. Instead of the 4 bones recommended below, put about 8 in the pot, use the marrow from 4 for the soup, and keep the other 4 to reheat for the hangover breakfast tomorrow.*

Requirements:

4 marrow-bones	2 leeks,
2 onions	4 cloves garlic
2 sticks celery	3 carrots
4 cups beef stock	3 sprigs thyme
1 tsp peppercorns	1 tsp allspice berries
$1/4$ cup chopped parsley.	

Instructions:

Put marrowbones in soup pot with skim of olive oil on bottom, then cover and roast at high heat for a few mins, turn bones, and roast again. Ends should be well browned, slightly burnt even. Douse with stock, chop the vegetables fairly finely, add them and herbs, simmer for 30 mins. Blow marrow from bones, add some stock to it, mix up to a slurry and add back to pot. Discard bones. Serve with sprinkling of parsley.

Debbie, our cook in the arctic, was horrified when Simeon cracked open the leg bones of a freshly killed caribou to eat the raw marrow. Two weeks later, he redeemed himself, temporarily, when he came back from a winter walkabout with a half frozen leg of caribou. After we'd dined on the superb stew she concocted, Debbie asked where he'd shot it.

"I didn't shoot it," Simeon replied. "A couple of days ago, I found it out there, already dead by something; so today I went back to cut off a leg for you to cook."

If I've told you once, I've told you a million times: don't exaggerate!

... he came back from a winter walkabout with a frozen leg of caribou.

Leek Soup

This is another of those dishes that just evolved, although I cannot take the blame for it: poor benighted Debbie from the Arctic camp had little in the pantry when a six day fog descended just as the supply plane was due. This ptarmigan based soup was one of her better concoctions; others involved sik-sik, which is a sort of large ground squirrel; and arctic hares, trapped by Simeon, our Inuit jack of all trades and her nemesis.

Requirements:

3 leeks	1 carrot
1 chicken carcase	3 sticks celery
2 squirts chicken-in-a-bottle	3 potatoes
1 tsp black peppercorns	1 tsp allspice berries
2 bay leaves	1 tsp fresh thyme
1 shake cayenne pepper	2 cloves garlic
6 green onions, as garnish.	1 beer

Don't ask how the beer found its way into a dry arctic camp!

Instructions:

Break bones of chicken carcase, especially leg and thigh bones, and boil in beer for 20 mins. Extract bones and discard after stripping off any flesh back into pot. Add sliced potatoes, boil another 20 mins, then mash. Add water, herbs and spices and other vegetables finely chopped and simmer for 30 mins. Garnish with chopped green onions just before serving.

Debbie was cooking for 10, this is throttled back to feed 4 to 6. With 5 loaves and a couple of fish, some have been known to feed more.

Medieval Prayer
"From ghoulies, from ghosties,
From long-leggedy creatures,
From things that go bump in the night
Protect us good Lord."

Chicken Broth

This started when a kamikaze francolin flew into my parked Landrover in the Zambezi valley (francolin are not very smart). The fowl was not even stunned, but its neck was wrung and it was plucked naked within a minute. However, the bird was so tough... here's what evolved.

Requirements:

Retain the bones from a roast chicken, the water in which potatoes for mashed potatoes, or rice, or vegetables were boiled, and left over gravy. The skin, the tail (the pope's nose) are also useful, and so, too, most especially is the cartilage.

1 onion	1 carrot
3 sticks celery	1 potato
1 tsp coriander seeds	1 tsp black peppercorns
2 squirts chicken-in-a-bottle	2 bay leaves
2 cloves garlic	1 lime, zest and juice.
1 tsp allspice berries	sprig of thyme leaves
$^1/_2$ cup cilantro	1 cup frozen peas

Instructions:

Break the bigger bones to let the marrow out, then boil the carcass and herbs for an hour at least in the reject water. Remove the bones, retaining any meat. Chop in the vegetables except peas and cilantro, to large chunks, bring back to the boil and boil gently for 20 mins. Add peas and finely chopped cilantro, return to boil for another 5 mins then serve.

Although I carried a shotgun, we were only allowed to shoot in self defence in the wilderness area where I was stationed in the Zambezi valley. You would not believe the fierce, naked aggression shown by the guinea fowl, partridge and grouse in that area. We ate well.

Learning Numbers

Play dominoes with your child from the earliest age: it helps with learning numbers and with arithmetic.

Potato Soup

This is an excellent basis for just about every decent cream soup there is, without using dairy products.

Requirements:

6-8 potatoes	4 cups chicken stock
1 leek	1 onion
1 green jalapeño	$^1/_2$ lb bacon
1 red pepper	2 medium carrots
2 sticks celery	handful of fresh parsley
salt and pepper	1 clove garlic

Instructions:

In a large soup pot, fry the bacon until very crispy, remove the bacon and crumble it, then set aside.

Depending on your taste and inclination, drain off some, all, or none, of the bacon grease.

While bacon is frying, chop onion, leek, celery, carrots, jalapeño and pepper very finely, then lightly fry them in the bacon grease. Douse with half chicken stock, crush in the garlic, then leave to simmer. In a separate pot, slice potatoes and boil for 20 minutes in chicken stock, then mash potatoes and stock together. Add to simmering vegetables. These impart not only a delightful flavour, but are attractive as flecks of red, orange and green in the ivory coloured soup. Add chopped parsley 5 minutes before serving. Just before serving sprinkle each bowl liberally with bacon fragments.

To convert this to asparagus soup, when you douse with chicken stock, chop up $^1/_2$ lb asparagus, or just dump in a can of asparagus. To convert to celery soup, chop up $^1/_2$ lb celery sticks. Cream of broccoli? Same deal, but also add a cup of sharp shredded cheddar. To ring the changes, you can even make fish soup with cubes of pollock.

Wine and Duct Tape

White wine is to a woman as duct tape is to a man, it fixes everything.

White wine is to a woman like duct tape is to a man,
it fixes everything.

Honduranians are lovable eccentrics. Ruthlessly exploited by corrupt governments run by US business interests for half a century, they have developed a healthy mistrust of all politicians, who are banned from seeking a second term in office. Their national hero is Don Quixote. My typical meal for almost two weeks working in the field was just tacos and beans; sometimes beans and tacos for variety.

DINNER RECIPES

My colleague Sigfriedo could never get his red-neck neighbour's yapping dog from using Sigfriedo's yard for a toilet. Neither hints nor direct complaints worked. Finally, siezing the dog crossing the fence, Sigfriedo headed inside. His irate neighbour immediately confronted him.

"I'm Filipino," Sigfriedo explained. "I'm making a curry. The dog will be ready in twenty minutes. Bring your wife, and we'll all enjoy it."

After that, the barking abated, but the crapping ceased.

"How I wish I were a dromedary,
On the plains of Timbuktu.
I would eat a missionary,
Bible, hymnbuk, prayerbuktu."

Ohmygawditsnearlydinnertimealready (*Omgindta*) Chilli

A standby on the rig, invented in collaboration with my son. It takes no time at all to prepare.

Requirements:

1 onion	1 can red kidney beans
1 pepper	1 can tomatoes
$^1/_2$ lb lean ground beef	garlic-plenty
chilli powder	splash of olive oil

Instructions:

In a saucepan, not a skillet, liven up chilli powder in oil, add beef, and fry until browned and crumbled. Chop and add onion pepper and garlic. Fry while you open cans. Add tomatoes; stir everything up while you wash canning sludge out of beans (*which cuts down their farting force*).

Add beans, allow everything to get hot, then enjoy. This is really good with fresh bread.

For years I had a lucrative contract with Canada's biggest oil company, until one annual spring conference in Kanaskis Village, when the CEO thanked several hundred contractors for a job well done, that had enhanced the company profits by thirty per cent...blah, blah, blah. At the end of his speech, he called for questions. It was that rare moment when one thinks of exactly the right thing to say, at the right time, not twenty minutes later. Unable to resist, I leapt to my feet, to ask:

"Does this mean that you will be doubling our day rate?"

The hall erupted in cheers! The CEO turned purple as he strode from the room. That company never hired me again, but for the next two days of the conference, everyone wanted to buy me a drink!

Salted Almonds

In 1 oz butter, fry $^1/_2$ lb almonds until lightly browned, drain, turn onto paper towel to dry and sprinkle with salt. Store in an airtight tin.

Roast Chicken

Serving roast chicken always gives the impression that you know your way about the kitchen. In fact, that's bull: it's dead simple. Follow these instructions; behaving as if you know what you're doing.

Requirements:

1 chicken, dressed trussed	2 sticks celery
6 potatoes, peeled, halved	1 onion
4 parsnips, young, peeled	1 lemon
4 carrots, young, peeled	4 shallots
6 cloves garlic	flour

salt & pepper, herbs to taste (thyme, bay leaves etc)

Instructions:

Lightly oil roasting pan; cover base with chopped onions and celery. Rub gut cavity with salt, pepper and herbs; into little slits in breast, back and thighs, insert slivers of garlic. Put lemon, leftover garlic, onion and celery into gut cavity. Place chicken on onion-celery base, surrounded by other ingredients. Cover, cook for 20 mins per lb, as follows: 30 mins at 500°F; 400 °F for time remaining; remove cover for last 15 mins. Remove chicken and allow to rest, move vegetables to covered entrée dishes. Move roaster to stovetop, add equal volume flour as there is hot drippings and cook till light brown with vigorous stirring. Add equal amount of wine, water or stock and boil with constant stirring until smooth. Pour into gravy boat. Carve the chicken.

My father was never allowed to carve, because when he and mother were newlyweds, entertaining for the first time, he hacked the chicken into quarters, one piece for each person present. Having lived as a bachelor for many years, and being a straightforward and pragmatic sort of man, he was unable to understand her chagrin.

Household Hint

A pinch of baking soda as you mash potatoes makes them more fluffy.

"If you do not like it, ignore it; or offer your own version in return." Salman
Rushdie

Ratatouille

This evokes a dual memory. For my spouse, she remembers her last vacation as
a child when her family rented a villa in the south of France. The 'bonne' made
this regularly and the smell of it cooking never fails to evoke happy memories of
those far off days. For me, when we were penniless, having only recently arrived
in Canada, I'd make this as a cheap meal with baked potatoes. Our daughter
accused me of trying to poison her with eggplant, which she detests, after her dog
Gigi refused the eggplant when she offered it.

Requirements:

1 of each: onion, red pepper, zucchini, eggplant, more garlic than you
can possibly need, and then some.

2 sticks celery	3 sprigs fresh thyme
bacon grease or olive oil	chicken-in-a-bottle

Instructions:

Into a saucepan in which great quantities of garlic are frying in a very little
bacon grease or olive oil (tasty vs. healthy), chop vegetables, add a squirt of
chicken-in-a-bottle and simmer until done. Tastes differ. Some like *al dente*,
some mushy. Either way it is good, eaten on its own, or with spuds, pasta,
rice, poached fish, grilled steak, or all the above!

Working on the rig, I made six times more than I could eat in a meal, having
the first portion al dente; *then two subsequent portions on the mushy side, as a*
vegetable. A third of the balance with chilli powder, salsa, beans and 4 oz fried
ground beef became chilli. *The next day a tablespoon curry paste, 4 oz cubed*
chicken thigh, some dried raisins and apricots transformed another third into
curry, and finally, on the last day, with a can of tomato paste, I created a fine
spaghetti sauce.

Surprise Spaghetti and Sausage for kids

Shove about a dozen raw spaghetti through $1/_2$ inch pieces of *kovbasa*, spaced every
4 inches; boil with normal pasta; serve with herb butter. The end result never failed
to tickle the children!

71

Irish Stew

This is the only occasion on which it is permissible to dish up turnips to humans. Normally, this delicacy should be reserved strictly for pigs: but an Irish stew without turnips is like sex without a partner. To be sure, it is possible, but it's just not the same; and there are those who say it will make you go blind. The glory of the dish is its simplicity.

Requirements:

lamb. Really it is not important what cut you use, scrag end or neck is as good as the finest rack or leg. Just cut it up into bite sized pieces.

potatoes, plenty, coarsely chopped

onions, chopped   carrots, chopped

leeks, washed and chopped   celery, chopped

1 turnip, finely diced   mashed potato to thicken

fresh green beans   peas, frozen

beef-in-a-bottle   beer-in-a-bottle

Instructions:

Brown the meat in the pot, then chuck in everything except the peas and mashed potato and leave to simmer. The ideal is a crock-pot, and leave it to fester until the meat just falls apart. About 10 minutes before serving, stir in the mashed potato to thicken, then add the peas.

Aunt Rosa was "different". When her six year old son Damian asked Santa for a sheep for Christmas, she bought him a real, live lamb. It then lived with them in their suburban home, until a bylaws officer told her that the animal must go. When she refused to comply, she and the now full grown sheep were driven out in the animal control van to the city pound, from which she had to be bailed out, and the sheep was sent to a local farm...or butcher.

Frying Bacon

Start bacon in a cold pan, never a hot one; fry slowly 6 or 7 mins.

... she and the now full grown sheep were driven
out in the animal control van to the city pound...

> **"It is not death that a man should fear, but should fear never beginning to live."**
> **Marcus Aurelius**

Pain Perdu

My wife's maternal grandmother, Mamy, mother of Bommie and Tantine, made this as a special treat for her granddaughters when she was babysitting them.

Requirements:

    2 slices white bread per person   1 or 2 eggs

    cassonade (Demerara sugar)

Instructions:

Soak slices of bread in beaten egg. Fry in pan until golden brown both sides. Serve warm with liberal quantities of cassonade sprinkled on top.

My son and his father are otherwise. They prefer to substitute ketchup for the cassonade. However, they are generally out of luck, as we keep no ketchup in the house.

An excellent substitute for the missing ketchup can be made with an onion, a clove or three of garlic and a large ripe tomato, fried up after dicing them finely, with a splash of herb butter and a little basil. Slop it on top of the French toast.

It always amuses me that in French the bread is lost, whereas in English the bread is French. It's similar with a condom, which is known to the Brits as "a French letter" and to the French as "l'imperméable anglais" (the English raincoat)!

Cream of Tartar

The baobab tree always looked upside down to me, with roots up in the air. The fruit is the size of an American football, packed with cream of tartar. Outside their native African lowveld, the trees follow old slave trading routes.

It has significance to earth scientists, because it occurs in Africa, Madagascar and Western Australia (where they call it a boab); whether due to continental drift (the old idea of plate tectonics) or ocean drift is moot.

Generic Curry

This recipe evolved when I was at an army staging post where there'd be anywhere from 3 to 25 people at a meal, with no notice. I had an extensive spice locker; Sergeant Swando kept a garden; there was always a chicken or three to murder, so feeding them wasn't impossible.

Requirements: For 4-12 people:

1$^1/_2$ tsp of real curry powder per 2 people

1 onion per person	$^1/_2$ green pepper per person
1 clove garlic per person	1 tsp fresh ginger, crushed,
"quite a bit" of celery	parsley, bay leaves, thyme, basil
1 tblsp ground tumeric,	$^1/_2$ tsp each nutmeg, cloves

1 each aubergine (aka egg plant), courgette, (aka zucchini), potato (aka spud), tomato (aka tomato), etc.

1 tsp each ground cardamom, allspice berries, mustard, cumen, coriander, peppercorns (black, white, green).

1 lemon juice and zest	2 beers.
2 cups stock	1 fresh apple or pear, or both

$^1/_2$ cup dried fruit: dates, raisins, apricots etc.

Road Kill, chicken, gopher, hamster, cat, the neighbour's dog, raccoon, squirrel, possum or rabbit (*never skunk*): chopped in bite-sized pieces, preferably after removing feathers and hair.

Instructions:

Put olive oil & curry powder in pan to "bring the powder alive"; add all meat, turning it until almost done; douse the pan, and souse yourself with a beer each. Add fruit and vegetables then turn to just simmer at very low heat. Late in the proceedings, if you remember, throw in some yogurt, sour milk or ghee.

Wash it down with fruit juice or beer, never wine. Eat over rice with sambals of mango slices, chopped apple and onion, sliced bananas in lemon juice and sweet mango chutney.

To eliminate the smell of perspiration, take a shower.

Soufflé

This is my wife's very special recipe, which has evolved from having been made in kitchens the world over with few to nil gadgets.

Requirements:

Béchamel	**Dough**	per person
2 cups milk	2 eggs	
1 tblsp butter	1 white of egg	
$^3/_4$ cup flour	$^1/_3$ cup grated cheese	
spices to taste	pinch cream of tartar	
$^2/_3$ lb cooked (al dente), (or not!) asparagus tips		

Instructions: *The basis is thick béchamel sauce, made in the microwave while the dough itself is prepared.*

Grease a deep, round, oven proof dish.

Béchamel In a large microwaveable bowl, whisk flour and spices into the milk. Add butter, zap on high for 2 minutes, whisk and zap again for another 2 minutes. Keep doing this until contents are well mixed into a thick sauce.

Dough Preheat oven to 380°F. Separate eggs and beat whites with cream of tartar until stiff. When béchamel is ready, whisk in egg yolks one at a time, then add cheese, folding it into béchamel. Line soufflé dish with asparagus. Now, without beating, fold beaten egg whites into béchamel mixture; pour into soufflé dish, and bake in hot oven for ±45 minutes. Soufflé is ready when fluffy and golden brown. Serve immediately.

Remember the soufflé rule:

A soufflé is like royalty, it waits for no-one: diners wait for the soufflé.

Frying Sausages

When frying pork sausages, start them in a little water instead of fat. As the water boils, it starts cooking, and releases some fat from the sausage, which then fries in its own juices. Cover, because it spits.

Stealth Cauliflower

This is my wife's own concoction. It is an incredibly good camouflage, disguising cauliflower from even the most discriminating adolescent palate; which goes to prove that everything is better with bacon, or with cheese, and better yet with both. This works equally as a meal for two, or as a side dish for visitors, who never fail to be impressed.

Requirements:

1 cauliflower	3-4 medium potatoes
1 bunch green onions	$1^1/_2$ cups milk*
1 tblsp butter	$^3/_4$ lb bacon
4 tsp mayonnaise	1-2 tbsp flour

plenty of grated cheese, and some.

* you can substitute chicken stock for the milk

Instructions:

Line bottom of lightly oiled medium rectangular casserole dish with sliced potatoes, season with salt and pepper, then cover with cauliflower florets. Meanwhile, fry chopped bacon until crisp and set aside on paper towel to drain. Discard bacon grease. In a saucepan, fry chopped green onions in butter until soft, remove from heat and stir in flour, then stir in milk and return to heat, stirring constantly while sauce thickens, and continue cooking (but do not boil) for 2-3 mins. Remove from heat, stir in mayonnaise, and pour over cauliflower. Cover with bacon, then with grated cheese. Bake at 450°F for 30-45 mins until potatoes are tender, and cheese is golden and melted. Enjoy.

Discarding bacon drippings seemed so wasteful, particularly as it attracted ravens shredding our garbage bags, so I laid a rat trap for them. The sprung trap caught no raven, but the vandalism ceased. A week later our neighbour commented on the brutality of someone (my rat trap?) who had put a deep dent in their cat's snout. I never 'fessed up.

Household Hint

To loosen jar tops, run the hot tap over the jar and top for a few minutes. The metal top will expand more, and more rapidly, than the glass jar, making it easier to twist off.

Red Beans

I learnt this from Marella, wife of a farmer in Michoacán, when I was there with my mining partner, José. It is an approximation, because she just guessed the quantities, while I watched her!

Requirements:

1lb dry red beans

Some jalepeños, allspice berries

Celery, an onion, a red or green pepper

crushed garlic, and some more garlic.

A lump of lard, or bacon drippings (bacon grease)

Ham bone with some ham attached.

1 Polish Sausage (*Marella used chorizo, but I've adjusted it*)

Beef or chicken stock.

Instructions:

Put beans in a pot of water, and leave overnight. Toss out water, rinse beans, cover with water and get another large pot. Strip ham from bone. Slice sausage, dice ham, toss them, with bone, into second pot and fry them up in bacon grease to get a bit of colour onto the meat. Meanwhile dice onions, celery and peppers, and chuck them and garlic in with meat when it is browned, fry until onions are translucent and turning brown. Add spices, then turn heat right down and douse with the stock. Drain beans, then add them. Chuck all in & leave, stirring occasionally. The slower they cook, the better. A crock pot is the answer.

You can open a can of beans, and just add trimmings - it tastes the same. However, there is some satisfaction in going the campesino *way, starting from dried beans.*

José and I gave up the Mexican Venture after 'narcos' gunned down six young policemen near our claims: we figured we might be next.

Lemon Butter for Grilled Sole

Into 4 oz softened salted butter, mix the juice and zest of a lemon. Use to baste the fish while grilling.

Frikadelle

My mother used to make these, which she called keftedes, *because her Greek friend, Helena, made the same thing. I had always thought that the name* frikadelle *was Afrikaans, but our Danish friend, Solvejg put us right on that score. In effect, this recipe is my fusion version of the 3 originals.*

Requirements:

5 slices stale bread	2 tblsp milk
2 sprigs fresh thyme	1 clove garlic
2 good sprigs fresh mint	1 tsp salt
2 sprigs fresh oregano	1 onion
1 lb ground beef, lamb, or both	1 large egg
coarse black pepper	$^1/_2$ cup flour

Instructions:

Soak bread in milk in large bowl. Mince garlic, onion, herbs, salt, and pepper together until finely chopped, then add to bread and milk, with meat and eggs, and work in with hands. Roll into 1 inch balls, and coat with flour.

Best done by shaking gently in brown paper bag with flour.

Deep fry over medium heat in olive oil until browned, drain on paper towel.

If you skip the mint, it becomes less Greek... more South African... skip the herbs and garlic altogether, and use lean pork and or veal instead of the beef and lamb, to turn it more Scandewegian... and if you fry them in butter, more Danish... or bake them for 30 mins at 350°F and they're more Canadian, and therefore more healthy for you: but who wants it more healthy?

The versatility of these frikadelle-keftedes *is endless. Serve them hot, or cold with tsitsiki... or grainy mustard... or chutney...*

Helpful Hint

When baking stuffed tomatoes, put them in muffin tins or cup-cake forms on a baking tray. It stops them disintegrating.

"All animals are equal, but some animals are more equal than others." George Orwell

Rabbit Stew

My brother has a taste for rabbit stew; but, in the town to which he retired, the local butcher did not carry rabbit. Nothing daunted, brother went to the pet shop and bought one; slaughtering, cleaning and dressing it himself. He repeated this for a couple of months, until the pet shop owner enquired how the rabbits were. After my dear brother told him, in perfect sincerity, that they were delicious, but that the last one was a bit tough, he was banned forthwith from the pet store.

He now delights in phoning them to ask if they have rabbits, then asks: "fresh or frozen?"

<u>Requirements:</u>

1 rabbit (±3 lb)	2 cups diced carrots
6 small onions	3 diced potatoes
1 bay leaf	3 tblsp flour
$^1/_2$ cup chopped celery	1 tblsp finely cut parsley
1 tsp salt	1 beer

<u>Instructions:</u>

Simmer disjointed rabbit in beer with diced onions, celery, bay leaf, salt, in casserole dish for 2 hours. Add carrots & potatoes; continue cooking 20-30 mins until carrots are tender. Make thin paste with flour and water, and stir slowly into stew. When stew thickens, add parsley. Serve immediately.

When the town of Canmore appealed for suggestions to eliminate a rabbit infestation, I sent this recipe: they did not have the courtesy to respond. I experienced similar rudeness from an international lingerie company, which did not deign to reply to my application to be a bra fitter; for which I am eminently suited, as it would combine a job with my hobby.

To Catch A Rabbit

Place a lettuce leaf on a large rock, sprinkle with pepper. When bunny sniffs the lettuce, he'll sneeze, bashing his brains out on the rock.

... he was banned forthwith from the pet store.

Smokin' Salmon Spaghetti

This was a standby treat for us when we were "fresh off the boat", living hand-to-mouth, when each of us with two jobs, struggling to get by. Whoever arrived home first, man, woman or child, did the cooking. Thursdays were always particularly trying, as all four of us worked late, so Smokin' Salmon Spaghetti became the perennial Thursday fare.

It's simplicity itself, quick to make, and Oh! So good.

Requirements:

packet of spaghetti	splash of olive oil
4 oz frozen, smoked salmon.	knob of garlic butter
squeeze of chicken-in-a-bottle	

pasta aficionados will object that the oil stops the spaghetti from absorbing the sauce. If you're one of them, don't add it!

Instructions:

Boil a couple of pints of water, add the chicken-in-a-bottle and olive oil, dump in spaghetti, and boil for 8 mins. Drain, add the thawed salmon and a knob of garlic butter. Toss and serve.

Like so many immigrants, we arrived full of optimism; soon employed by a shyster for whom paying his employees was less important than living beyond his means at the right address...you know the tale.

When that president caught his fingers in the till, the bubble burst; the company evaporated, still owing us 3 months wages...so the kids found work: scooping ice-cream until she had frostbite; digging ditches until he had calluses on his blisters, and endless baby-sitting.

We adults found work: teaching French to receptionists, soldiers and undergraduates; drafting at an hourly rate, where an hour's work took a day; where technical specifications were typed with two fingers; struggling to suppress flat foreign accents; weeping with frustration at an unsympathetic labour exchange. We survived, sustained by a weekly treat of Smokin' Salmon Spaghetti...and hope.

Duct Tape
If you can't fix it with duct tape, you're not using enough

Every Friggen Night Spaghetti

As a student, I shared an apartment with another penniless undergraduate, Edgar. Whenever it was his turn to cook, he produced this one single contribution to the culinary arts, always exactly the same. It is almost elegant in its lack of sophistication. Don't fret about accuracy, Edgar didn't: a box is a box, a package is a package, some is some.

Requirements:

a box spaghetti	some very ripe tomatoes
a package pork sausages.	a large onion
some bacon grease.	some salt

Instructions:

Place bacon grease in hot skillet. Put large pot of water on high, add salt. Without peeling, cut onion vertically into quadrants, root side down, *do not cut right through.* Toss entire onion into the hot oil to fry. After one minute, using the knife, flick out skin and roots of onion. *Edgar did this as one piece, every time, flicking it across the kitchen into the sink, with unerring accuracy.*

Take a tomato in one hand, hold over skillet and squeeze sharply to disintegrate on top of frying onion pieces. Repeat with second tomato. *I challenge anyone to achieve this without squirting tomato juice over half the kitchen. Edgar never splashed any where!*

Cut last centimetre off package of sausages, to open them all, then squeeze out contents from each individual sausage into skillet, discarding skins. Stir aimlessly with knife. Empty contents of spaghetti box into water, boil 8 minutes, drain, and dump contents of skillet into spaghetti pot.

Edgar was a miracle of nature. A carpenter by trade, at age 37 he decided to change profession, starting as an undergraduate, ending as a well respected college professor, with a doctorate in philosophy, majoring in mathematics.

To Boil an Egg

Use boiling water.

"**Gossip is what no one claims to like, but everyone enjoys.**" Joseph Conrad

---

Impossible Chicken Pie

'They ain't no blood relatives', but we are proud to call family Jeanie* and Joe*, who were so unbelievably kind to us when we arrived 'fresh off the boat'. Joe never fails to introduce us as 'the folk from Waycross...way 'cross the sea, that is'. Now retired, the flying Js (including deaf dog) tour Colorado and New Mexico endlessly in their 'Vanilla Moose', a well preserved old Suburban, towing 'the tin tepee', an equally well preserved Airstream. This is Jeannie's recipe.

<u>Requirements:</u>

1 broiler chicken, dismembered	2 cups water
1 x 6 oz can tomato paste	2 x $^1/_2$ tsp salt
2 x $^1/_2$ cup mozzarella cheese	2 eggs
1 tsp oregano leaves	1 tsp basil leaves
$^1/_2$ cup small curd cottage cheese	1 cup milk
$^1/_2$ cup prepared biscuit mix	$^1/_2$ tsp pepper

<u>Instructions:</u>

Boil chicken in water for 20mins with $^1/_2$ tsp of salt, skin and debone it, cut into bite sized chunks. Put in large bowl, mix in tomato paste, herbs and $^1/_2$ cup cheese. Spread cottage cheese over base of lightly oiled large quiche dish, then cover with chicken mix. Put everything else except second $^1/_2$ cup cheese into the bowl, beat it, and pour over the top. Bake at 350°F for 30 mins, sprinkle top with second cheese and finish under the grill.

Jeannie prefers not to make things; she'd sooner brag: "I bought it myself!" She's the expert at finding bargains on the clearance racks, but shopping time never extends too far into the afternoon, regardless of the bargains on offer, as that might intrude into 'sippies time'!

* I've not changed their names - their selfless kindness to four homeless immigrants deserves to be recognized.

Uninspired Frosting

A very tasty and attractive frosting can be made by stirring raspberry jam into creamed unsalted butter and icing sugar.

FISH DISHES

Chaap-chaap Fish	86
Sardines on Toast	88
Marinara Sauce	89
Shrimp Souvlaki	90
Moule Casserole	92
Comfort Food Salmon	93
Tuna Casserole	94

Good food creates its own ambiance.

Just outside Savannah, Georgia, there is a restaurant that serves only fresh steamed prawns by the pail, dumped onto the newsprint that serves as tablecloth: no cutlery, no crockery. When I asked for a wine list, the waitress told me there was none, but she assured me that they did indeed serve wine.

"What wines do you have?" I asked.

"Well, there's your red; and then there's your white," she replied.

She was serious.

"Two glasses of your red, please, for the ladies."

"No glasses, honey; plastic disposable cups only."

"Uh-huh. Two cups of red then, and my friend and I will have a beer each, please,"

"Unless it's Bud," Joe interjected, "in which case I'll have wine."

The waitress drew back, a pained expression of mortal offence clouding her face.

"This is a decent establishment, honey," she sniffed. "We don't serve Bud."

The wine was exceptional; the beer even better, from a local microbrewery. Seldom have we eaten so well, rarely have we had such an enjoyable meal. For the record, the restaurant is Despositos.

Instant "At-a-Pinch" Apricot Chutney

Chop up 5 tablespoons of chunky apricot jam, add salt, pepper and hot sauce, thin with vinegar

Chaap-Chaap Fish

This collaboration comes from my son and me, sitting interminable gas wells in northern BC. It is of the same genre as Omgindta Chilli, taking minimum effort and time: hence "Chaap-chaap", pidgin for 'hurry'.

It wasn't Debbie doing the cooking, 'twas I. When I took out the garbage, I forgot to replace my reading glasses with regular specs, so I was effectively blind. I tossed the garbage into the trash trailer, where it scared the bejasus out of a young cinnamon bear, which took off at high port, scaring the bejasus out of me.

<u>Requirements</u>: (for about 2 or 3 people)

1 brick frozen cod	1 onion
1 box frozen peas	2 sticks celery
chicken-in-a-bottle	5 to 7 potatoes
milk and butter	

<u>Instructions:</u>

Put 2 saucepans of water on to boil. Chop onions and celery into one, chop potatoes into the other, with a squeeze of chicken-in-a-bottle in each. When everything has been boiling 5 mins, put the frozen cod in with the onions, it will stop boiling, then gradually heat up again; when it has been boiling another 5 mins, add frozen peas, bring back to the boil for another 5 mins. At this time, potatoes will be done, remove and drain.

(I retain the liquid, and drink it as soup)

Mash together with butter and milk, drain the other and it's all ready to eat simultaneously, about 25 mins from start.

My grandfather held that to serve peas without mashed potatoes was ill mannered, verging on barbarism, showing lack of planning: one needs the potatoes to ensure that the peas stayed on the fork.

Peas

I eat my peas with honey, I've done it all my life,
It makes the peas taste funny, but it sticks 'em to my knife.

I eat my peas with honey, I've done it all my life,
It makes my peas taste funny, but it sticks 'em to my knife.

I offer this, my late father's remarkably versatile recipe!

One can substitute a can of baked beans instead of the sardines, or a can of tuna, or a can of chilli, or salmon, even a few slices of cheese, or slices of raw onion, or both. You can even do away with the toast-but you have to have one or the other, as sardine-free, bread-free sardines-on-toast is not a substantial meal on its own.

Sardines-on-Toast

This reminds me of Sir Harry Lauder, that turn of the 19-20th century singer, comedian and song writer, who sang of his greatest desire when his wife went away to visit her mother: to eat a can of sardines.

Requirements:

    1 can sardines   2 slices bread

Instructions:

Open the can of sardines. Drain off fluid. Toast bread. Dump sardines on toast. Eat and enjoy.

If desired, you can fluff it up with chopped onions, celery, garlic, banana peppers. My father didn't bother with such niceties.

The quintessential kilted Scottish singer-songwriter and comedian, Sir Harry was a truly tragic figure, whose only son was killed in the trenches in the first world war, from which the old fellow never recovered. He wrote his most lasting song in memory of the lad: "Keep Right on to the End of the Road", which became a favourite of my grandfather, who lost two brothers in that terrible conflict.

Cooking Rice

We learnt this in the army. Tie 1 cup of dry rice in a plastic bag, prick liberally, toss into boiling salted water for 20-30 mins. Perfect every time: literally, every time! Alternatively put 1 cup of rice, 2 cups of chicken broth, or of water with 2 squirts of chicken-in-a-bottle, a dollop of butter and 1 tsp lemon juice in the microwave for 5 mins, fork over, then 20mins and rest. Perfect every time, except that we had no microwave when we were on patrol in the bush!

> **"The weak can never forgive. Forgiveness is the attribute of the strong."**
> **Mohandas Gandhi**

Marinara Sauce

This is a joint development by our son and daughter. Take heart younger parents, the first thirty years of parenthood are the worst.

Requirements:

1 small onion	4 cloves garlic, crushed
1 tsp herb butter	6 Roma tomatoes, diced
1 portabella mushroom	$^1/_2$ cup parsley, chopped fine
1 x 6 oz can tomato paste	

Instructions:

Fry onions and garlic in herb butter until onions are translucent. Add tomatoes, mushrooms and tomato paste. Fill tomato paste can with water and add. Simmer for 15 minutes. Add parsley and serve over pasta.

An interesting adjustment to this basic recipe is to add to the simmering broth a $^1/_2$ lb bag of assorted *fruits-de-mer* about 5 mins before serving. Thaw the *fruits-de-mer* before adding them. The purists may disagree, but I like a shot of Tabasco in my Marinara, especially with the seafood.

My spouse adores seafood...except for "leggedy creatures". To disguise the squids and little octopi in these fruits-de-mer, I snip them up into small pieces... with limited success. She was easier to fool before her cataract surgery.

Some years ago, on holiday in South Carolina, we stopped at a restaurant famous for soft shell crab hoagies, where they made the mistake of leaving the legs hanging out of the hot fresh bread roll. Wife refused point blank to touch it.

This was not all bad news: I had two.

Cure For Warts

According to Huck Finn:

"heave a dead cat after a grave robber:

'. . . and say: "Devil follow corpse, cat follow devil, warts follow cat, I'm done with ye!" That'll fetch any wart'."

Shrimp Souvlaki

These never fail to impress at a barbeque. Serve these with a dip of melted garlic butter; accompanied by fresh garden salads on the deck on a warm summer evening. They just slide down the gullet with an ice cold Portuguese rosé wine.

Requirements:

1 lb prawns (21-25 count)	1 clove garlic
1 cup fresh dill	1 cup chardonnay
zest of 1 lime	juice of 2 limes

Instructions:

Peel shrimps, marinade for 20 mins in chopped dill, crushed garlic, wine, lime juice and zest. Meanwhile soak 5 or 6 wooden skewers in water. String the prawns onto the skewers...grill over lump hardwood charcoal embers until light pink (a couple or three minutes, maximum)

This derives from a beach barbeque I attended at the end of a project in Luderitzbucht, Namibia. Half a dozen Rehoboth Baster fishermen were employed pulling fresh Atlantic crayfish from the icy surf, to be grilled on the beach by their wives for the company guests. By far the best food served, however, was fresh prawns on skewers that wallowed in a marinade in a shallow porcelain bowl that I'll swear started life as a hospital chamber-pot. As one passed along selecting delicacies from the groaning buffet, sipping iced South African Steen* wine, a skewer or two would be lifted onto the charcoal "braai", while you waited the few moments it took to grill them. Very civilized, and unbelievably delicious.

The Baster lady tending the prawns kindly gave me the marinade recipe verbally in mixed Afrikaans-Deutsche, and by trial and error this has evolved from what I recollect of our conversation; but I never did find another bedpan to recapture the ambiance.

*steen is the local name for chenin blanc

The First Rule Of The Home Handyman

If it moves but shouldn't, duct tape it: if it should but doesn't; use WD40.

By far the best food served, however, were fresh prawns on skewers that wallowed in a marinade in a shallow porcelain bowl that I'll swear started life as a hospital chamber pot.

Moule Casserole

There is little simpler, nor more typically Belgian. When the kids were just picaninnies, *on a seaside vacation with little money, at low tide, dad clambered down to cut mussels from the rocks, which son ferried to his sister on the beach, who, in turn, carted their little pails back up to mother, waiting with the pot.*

Requirements:

5 cloves garlic	2 onions
4 sticks celery	dash or 2 olive oil
pepper corns	allspice berries
sprig fresh thyme	
and of course, several lbs of mussels	

Instructions:

In a pot of 50:50 sea and fresh water, chop the onions, garlic and celery; add a dash of olive oil and herbs. When boiling, add plenty of fresh, live mussels, boil for 5 minutes. Serve drained, with hot crisp fries on the side. Enjoy with chilled *vinho verde* or ice cold dry rosé.

Even living on the prairies, this is a favourite at our weekly family dinner. Without seawater in Calgary, use cheap white wine, to make excellent broth, with a squirt of chicken-in-a-bottle.

> **One caveat: if any mussel is open before they're cooked, reject it; if any are closed after cooking, reject them also. If there's more than five rejects in a bag, eat none, and never use that fishmonger again!**

Cure For Warts

According to Tom Sawyer:

"just as it's midnight, you back up against a stump and jam your hand in and say:
'Barley-corn, barley-corn, injun meal shorts,
Spunk-water, spunk-water, swaller them warts.'"

Comfort food Salmon

Driven by the cooking channels on television, people seem to forget that the essence of good cooking remains simplicity. There is no need for the fancy-smancy sauces and glazes that the competing chefs conjure to titivate jaded palates. Try this gourmet food at its greatest, which requires little more energy than you usually have on a Tuesday when faced with creating dinner, for two in this case.

Requirements:

2 frozen salmon filets ($^1/_2$ lb)	3-4 small carrots
1 cup frozen peas	6 potatoes
4 good shakes dried dill	chicken-in-a-bottle
2 sticks celery	1 onion
whole milk	garlic butter

Instructions:

Slice carrots and boil with splash of chicken-in-a-bottle for 15 mins, then add peas, boil another 5 mins, drain, add knob herb butter. Ready to serve.

Slice potatoes, boil with splash of chicken-in-a-bottle for 18 mins, mash with herb butter and a little milk. Ready to serve.

Cover base of individual dishes with bed of diced celery and onions and a dab of herb butter. Lay frozen salmon, skin side down, on bed, cover with dill and a light squeeze of chicken-in-a-bottle, seal in seran wrap and nuke in microwave for 7-8 mins.

This takes half an hour to prepare and cook. When done, it not only looks good on the plate, it also smells and tastes really good, and it's a healthy meal. The six potatoes are way more than necessary for the meal: that's because you should always have a stash of mashed potatoes to use for thickening in a stew or soup. Cooking gurus will criticise the use of a microwave; but then, they are not doing the cooking for us, are they? Likewise, those same aficionados will protest at the salmon being overcooked... so if that's your gripe, cut the time down: not a problem!

Household Hint

To prevent silver from tarnishing, good luck!

Tuna Casserole

This was another cheap and simple stand-by meal for us when we were fresh in the country. The attraction lies in the simplicity of preparation. In truth, it should be called tuna-flavoured potato casserole: but what's in a name?

Requirements:

6 potatoes	1 banana pepper
3 carrots	1 cup frozen peas
2 onions	1 tblsp fresh thyme leaves
1 red pepper	chicken-in-a-bottle
1 or 2 cans tuna	crushed garlic to taste
1 cup Chardonnay	3 tomatoes

Instructions:

Dice everything, chuck it all in a crock pot and leave to simmer until the carrots are done (30 minutes or longer). Enjoy.

Inspiration for this dish came indirectly from poor benighted Debbie, the Arctic cook, who made something like this on her "lazy" days. One such day arose when she hitched a ride with "Rambo" the helicopter pilot to Arviat, an Innu fishing hamlet on the west coast of Hudson Bay. There was a beluga maturing on the shore, whose memorable odour, discernable from at least a kilometre from the place, started her retching. Then the sight of it, surrounded by the entire village population munching on marginally fresh muktuk, the raw blubber, as it was flensed from the whale's flanks, proved too much. She threw up in the chopper. Rambo flew her back to camp immediately, then hosed down the cockpit, muttering to himself. He refused to have her in his chopper again; which was as well, because Debbie refused to fly in it.

We made ourselves tuna casserole for dinner that night.

Visitors

House guests are very like fish. They are very welcome when they are freshly arrived, but they begin to stink after three days.

Rambo, the pilot, flew her back immediately,
then hosed down the cockpit, muttering to himself.

MISCELLANEOUS

The country of our birth was landlocked. During the civil war, sardines were difficult to acquire, so they became a luxury item. Hindu troops were issued them in their ration packs, so I'd trade my bully-beef with the black troops for their nyema beans, then the beans for sardines from the vegetarian Hindus. Did the military really regard pilchards as vegetables? I wonder.

My platoon sergeant, Swando, was always on the lookout for a deal. He once "liberated" a case of 'K' rations, half of which we traded for a box of salamis; and half of the salamis we exchanged at a brewery for two dozen of their wares. The other half of the rations went to a baker, who gave us fresh bread in return, half of which we traded for corn and fresh vegetables. For three days thereafter, our platoon ate like kings, before we had to go foraging again.

I never did discover why those civilians wanted the 'K' rations. They were horrible at best.

Putsi **maggots**

If you or your family have *putsi* maggots, do not squeeze the lump. Wait another day or two, until you can see the little black eyes, then a dab of Vaseline will bring the maggot wriggling out.

Bachelor's Breakfast

Requirements:

2 dozen eggs	1 lb lard	salt
1 can opener	fork	pepper
mixing bowl	tub Vaseline	Tabasco
2 skillets	stove	4 kitchen towels
emery paper	spray can WD 40	1 can tuna

Instructions:

Turn all knobs on stove clockwise to maximum extent; wait until all rings turn cherry red, then turn off all but two.

This ensures that you can identify on which rings to place the frying pan for maximum efficiency. If no ring turns red, listen carefully for faint hissing sound, indicating stove is on gas, not electricity: turn all knobs counter-clockwise and evacuate premises immediately. Do not smoke for at least two blocks. Order takeout. If stove is electric, all is well.

Crack egg on mixing bowl. Scrape mess off countertop. Start again. Scrape up mess again. Mash remaining eggs in mixing bowl with can of tuna. Using fork, flick out larger pieces of shell. Stir briskly, adding salt, pepper and Tabasco to taste. Pour half batter into skillet, place on stove. When smoke appears from beneath eggs (*indicates lack of lubrication*), remove and place skillet in sink in water. Preheat reserve skillet on stove while you clean first skillet with emery paper. Drop lump of lard on second skillet.

Wipe boiling fat from face and arms with kitchen towels and grope for Vaseline, applying liberally to affected body parts.

Abandon omelette idea. Open can of tuna.

And the WD-40? Always have some handy, you never know when, and for what, it will be needed.

Household Hint

To get the smell of fish off your hands, rub them with coffee grounds: to get the smell of coffee off your hands, rub them in fish.

Fritters

This is my grandmother's recipe for the Scots answer to doughnuts or beignets, but with a difference: if you stir into the batter lumps of fruit, like apples or peaches, bananas or pineapple, they make a pleasant and different dessert. Substitute some of the flour with cooked pumpkin, sweet potato or potatoes, and there you have another way to disguise leftovers. Add a can of creamed corn, or a cupful of cooked corn kernels for sweet corn fritters. Altogether, a remarkably versatile recipe!

During the Katanga crisis in 1960, when my wife was in a refugee camp, she was fed on pumpkin, pumpkin, and more pumpkin. To this day, over half a century later, she cannot look a pumpkin in the eye... although she has been tempted by a pumpkin fritter.

Requirements:

2 eggs	$^1/_2$ cup milk
1 cup flour	2 tsp baking powder
1 tsp oil or bacon dripping	pinch salt

Instructions:

Rub the lard into the flour, salt and baking powder mixture. In a separate bowl, beat 2 eggs, then stir in the milk, followed by the dry ingredients mixture. Add the fruit or vegetables. Deep fry in hot oil (375°F) until brown, drain and serve with syrup (fruit) or gravy (vegetables), or with nothing.

This has transmogrified from a treat for us as kids, when our parents were "going out", into a breakfast dish served with crispy bacon and eggs over-easy on the morning after a barbeque party. Some onions fried with or in the fritters makes them a magical alternative to hash browns. Trust me; even the reddest of southwest rednecks will trade their biscuits and gravy for sweet corn fritters with onions.

Take A Little Wine For Your Stomach's Sake

The medical profession assures us that a glass of red wine per day is excellent for our health. How much better, then, is an entire bottleful?

Malaxé

This is always a hit at any party, for folk of any age: this remains my father-in-law's greatest contribution to the culinary art, served only on 'holidays and holy days' as it is the original artery clogger. Do use decent port, as the cheap ersatz plonk produced elsewhere in the world is an affront to the senses. It also fails to keep the mixture creamy. Be sure to serve with radishes, gherkins, green onions, pickled onions and plenty of very fresh baguette. Wash down with full bodied claret or port.

Requirements:

    4 oz Danish blue cheese

    4 oz cream cheese *natural is best, not the plastic muck*

    4 oz unsalted butter

    $^1/_2$ cup ruby port wine *or Oloroso sherry or Madeira.*

Instructions:

Stand ingredients out on kitchen counter for at least a couple of hours to get everything to room temperature and soft. *Whatever you do, do not be tempted to speed things up by zapping them, even momentarily, in the microwave.* Crumble blue cheese into cream cheese. then beat in butter to a smooth consistency. Slowly beat in port. For some strange reason, it tastes better beaten by hand. The mixture absorbs far more wine than you think possible. Leave to stand for a few hours.

During the civil war in the old country, when luxuries were difficult to find, we acquired a fine Stilton, a bottle of old malt whisky, and a jar of caviar. What else to do, but organize a party for Saturday night.... but the chef, specially hired for the occasion, threw out the Stilton, because it was "going off", fed the caviar to the cat and drank all the whisky.

We didn't even have a cat!

Egg Yolk in Sauce

Stir each yolk into an egg-cupful of cream, then stir into the sauce. That way, the yolk will not curdle as it is added to the hot mixture.

> "I often wonder what the vintners buy, one half so precious as the goods they sell." Omar Khayyam

---

Cottage Cheese

Ours was a mixed farm. While my grandmother ran poultry (chickens, ducks and even turkeys for a while) and a market garden, my grandfather's interests lay in pigs; for he followed Churchill's view: "Dogs look up to us. Cats look down on us. Pigs treat us as equals". My mother and father ran sheep and a small dairy herd, but it was my grandmother who really "did" the dairying. This comes from her.

Requirements:

4 cups or more of whole milk	salt and pepper

Instructions:

Skim cream off and set aside. Place milk in enamel bowl in bain marie at low heat until curds separate from whey, which could be a couple of hours to a day. Drain through cheesecloth *(who'd have thought, eh?)*; hang over sink to drain until quite solid feeling. Empty bag into bowl, work in cream removed earlier. If too stiff, add a little top milk. Serve with salads or on crackers.

Grandmother's fearsome Holstein bull, Induna, terrified everyone, but became so attached to my brother, then aged about ten, that Induna followed him around like a puppy.

Wine Pairings

Before the meal:	dry sherry or vermouth
with fish:	dry white wine
with oysters, shell fish	sparkling white wine
with prawns, lobster	off dry white or sparkling wine
with entrees	light red or rosé
with poultry	fine dry white
with game birds	light red
with red meat, venison	full bodied red
with dessert	sparkling wine or sweet white wine
with cheese	port or cream sherry
with coffee	liqueur or brandy

Churchill's view "Dogs look up at us. Cats look down on us.
Pigs treat us as equals.".

Mayonnaise

This comes from Tante Claire, known throughout the family as Tantine, who lives in Uccles, Bruxelles. She taught it to my wife when we visited them on our honeymoon. In turn, my spouse then taught it to her mother, known as Bonne-Maman or Bommie to the kids. Bommie took a few months, then taught it back to my wife.

When dining out, Tantine's favourite meal is filet américain *on bread with mayonnaise. It's known as* toast cannibal *in Belgium.*

Requirements:

1 tsp mustard powder	yolk of 1 egg
as much olive oil as necessary	pinch of salt
Juice of $^1/_2$ lemon	

(or an entire lemon, depending on whether it is juicy or not)

Instructions:

Beat lemon juice, salt, mustard and egg yolk until frothy; then, constantly beating enthusiastically, add olive oil drop by drop until mayonnaise is thick and creamy. Substitute mustard with horseradish, tomato paste, or curry powder to give different tastes, as required.

Oncle Jacques, Tantine's late husband was a rare breed: he was one of the last Walloons who could speak the Walloon language fluently. Like every true Belgian, Jacques enjoyed his beer. He'd always order two Jupilers to start, then as he finished the second would announce: "Jamais deux, sans trois." and order a third. Belgium boasts 850 different beers. When we first met, I gave him a Davy Crockett coonskin hat; thereafter he wore it every time he took me on a "beer safari", to ensure that I tasted as many different local beers as possible.

I still have just under 500 beers to go, to taste them all.

Chopping Parsley

My mother-in-law produced this magnificent idea. Put parsley sprigs in a tea cup, then use a small pair of kitchen scissors to snip, snip, snip until the parsley is finely chopped. It's very rapid.

Ginger Beer

My brother and grandmother collaborated brewing this moonshine. They were enthusiastic, but were neither of them proficient, as they lacked the patience to wait before they bottled it.

Grannie's brewing escapades were the stuff of legend. She blew up the dairy, when she put still fermenting hooch bottles in the earthenware milk cooling trough. Her favourite tipple was gin and ginger beer. Once, we could not bathe indoors for a week, when she made mead in the bathtub.

Requirements:

1 gallon water.	2 inches fresh ginger root.
1 cake baker's yeast	3 cups Demerara sugar,
handful of raisins	

Instructions:

Resurrect yeast overnight with 1 tblsp sugar in a cup of tepid water. Heat other water to boiling, add sugar, remove from heat as sugar dissolves. Pound ginger root in a pestle and mortar, and wash it whole into liquid. Allow to cool, add yeast mixture, cover and leave in a warm place 48 hours. Drop a couple of raisins into each bottle and fill with ginger beer. The raisins will presently rise to the top, at which time put bottles in the fridge for a few hours.

Do not close the bottles until the fermentation is almost over, as you risk repeating Grannie's disaster.

My eccentric grandfather was very careful to select the glass with the right 'ping' when flicked. After turning the glass delicately, to ensure that exactly 5 shots of 'pink' (bitters) were evenly distributed, he slopped in two fingers of any old gin, two lumps of ice and a squirt of soda. Nearing the end of his time, Grandfather was instructed to limit his gin to just one tot a day. He followed the directive, on average, in his own fashion, which was to have half a tot daily, then catch up the balance over the week-end.

If your child has an argument with a skunk, get rid of the child: you'll never get the stink out.

"I have learned silence from the talkative, toleration from the intolerant, and kindness from the unkind." Khalil Gibran

---

Fruit Pizza

It is with affection that we recall Easter in Leslieville, soon after we immigrated, when a family of strangers, Justin*, his wife "Raggedy" Anne*, and their twins Melody* and Heather* took us into their home, their hearts, and their family. Easter dinner was a wiener roast (no-one was wealthy then). This is the twins' recipe for the dessert that followed.

<u>Requirements:</u>

Crust	1 cup flour	3 tblsp brown sugar
	2 tblsp icing sugar	$^1/_2$ cup softened butter
Topping	$^2/_3$ lb cream cheese	$^1/_2$ cup white sugar
	1 tsp vanilla essence	
	fruit-strawberries, peaches, blueberries, bananas, etc.	
Glaze	1 cup apricot jam	1 tblsp water

<u>Instructions:</u>

Crust Mix all ingredients in bowl until it forms a ball. press into bottom of a pizza pan. Bake at 350°F for 10-15 mins. Set aside to cool.

Topping Beat together cheese, sugar and vanilla. Spread on crust. Arrange fruit on the top

Glaze Mix water and jam together, then either drizzle onto fruit, or rub through sieve over fruit.

We were introduced to the concept of a winter picnic by these folk. Apart from a blanket of snow in the mountains, all that is required is a humungous thermos of hot coffee, a dead chicken, some bread rolls, an ability to laugh at misfortune, and friends with a desire to have fun.

I still have the plank with "A Little Hope" inscribed on it that they gave me that first Christmas.

*These names have not been changed because of their humanity and generosity to this miserable family of immigrants.

Glassware

Rinse glasses in warm water into which a teaspoonful of ammonia has been added. The glass will sparkle like new.

Crème Caramel

You need a 2" deep ceramic dish for both stovetop and oven that can fit into a shallow roasting pan half filled with water.

Requirements:

caramel	crème	
3 tblsp sugar	4 cups whole milk	3 egg whites
2 tblsp water	4 egg yolks	$^1/_2$ cup sugar
	vanilla to taste	

Put roasting pan and water in the oven at 400°F.

Instructions:

Caramel

In the corning ware dish, on the stove top, put the sugar and water, and stir until the sugar crystallizes, liquefies, then starts to brown. This is critical, as the syrup hardens rapidly and will burn, so get the dish off the stove before that happens.

Crème

Heat, but do not boil, milk and vanilla in saucepan. In a bowl, beat together sugar and eggs until pale yellow and frothy; pour milk into egg mix, then pour the mixture over the caramel. Do not stir. Place dish in water bath in oven, and bake for ±45mins until brown on top and firm when skewer inserted. Cool then chill in fridge before serving.

I made two critical errors very early in our marriage. My wife told me that, should I ever dislike something she had cooked, I was to tell her immediately… and I did. Naïvely, when she asked how I was enjoying the crème caramel, I replied that it was lumpy (which it was). My first error was to say this; my greater error was that it was on the first occasion she was entertaining my parents to dinner. Divorce was only narrowly averted.

Man and Beast

A man behaving like a beast, does not surprise me in the least,
But nothing is more frightful than, a beast behaving like a man.

ETHNIC FOOD

About 30 miles from the mine where I was working, a run-down drive-in cinema was taken over by an Dayal, a hardworking entrepreneur, who cleaned it, gave it a lick of paint, dropped the price of admission, and put mother, mother-in-law and wife in the kitchen. Unlike most cinemas, there were two intermissions, and an ice cold beer (from under the counter), to wash down the most exquisite curry dishes imaginable.

The fame of the drive-in soon spread, drawing folk from 60 miles away, to enjoy food like none other. Not for us mere popcorn and liquorice twizzlers at our movies. Oh No! We enjoyed papadams and samoosas at the first intermission, then a good chicken vindaloo or Madras curried lamb with mouth-watering sambals at the second intermission.

In time, the movie itself became irrelevant, and folk merely came for the food...until some overzealous bylaws officer closed the drive-in because Dayal was serving alcohol without a liquor license.

Sit transit Gloria mundi!

If an investment opportunity seems too good to be true, it probably is.

Carbonnade Flamande

This real comfort food for cold winter nights is another quintessential Belgian dish. In so many other dishes where one uses beer, the quality of the beer matters little; but here you must use good dark brown ale instead of a light generic lager or pilsner.

Requirements:

Brown paper packet.	$^{1}/_{2}$ cup flour
2 tblsp beef dripping	salt
2 large onions, coarsely chopped	pepper
4 carrots, coarsely sliced	thyme
$^{1}/_{2}$ lb good, fat free stewing beef, coarsely chopped	
potatoes coarsely chopped (plenty, and then some)	
1 stick celery, coarsely chopped	1 or 2 dark ales

Instructions:

Spice and herb the flour in the paper bag, add the meat, and give it a good shaking to coat every piece with spiced flour. heat the dripping in a cast iron pot on the stovetop, drop in the floured beef and fry, constantly stirring to form a good thick brown roux. The darker brown the better, but *do not burn*. Pour in the beer, turn down the heat and add the vegetables to just simmering for as long as it takes. Serve with chilled dark ale.

In Namur, my wife's grandfather insisted we hit the local pub for a beer and bowl of Carbonnade Flamande. Delicious as the stew was, delightful as the house beer tasted, these were not the main attractions of the public house. Occupying a central display cabinet was 'le pisspot de Napoléon' which the patron's ancestor had "liberated" from the abandoned imperial coach after the battle of Waterloo.

Butternut Squash

Steam a cut-up squash until tender, then purée with sour cream and butter until smooth. Sprinkle with salt, pepper and chopped chives.

"Begin at the beginning and go on till you come to the end: then stop." Lewis Carroll

---

Bacalhau na Batatas

The Portuguese colony of Moçambique was an exotic Mediterranean vacation destination when we were kids, with a cuisine as interesting and unusual as their language and culture. For us it meant only prawns, langustine and galinhos piripiri, *and only with Julia (née Mary) in Lisboa did we learn of* sardinhos, polvos, lulas, *and* bacalhau. *Here's my interpretation of one such dish.*

<u>Requirements:</u>

2 potatoes	$^1/_2$ lb frozen cod
2 tomatoes	1 small eggplant
1 green pepper	1 large onion
1 cup frozen peas	3 good shakes Tabasco
1 squirt chicken-in-a-bottle	2 good sprigs thyme
1 tsp peppercorns	1 tsp allspice berries

<u>Instructions:</u>

Into an ovenware casserole, put a splash of olive oil, then cover base with thickly cut onion slices, then potato slices, then the cod fillets, then eggplant, green pepper and tomato. Toss in all the rest; shove it in the oven for about an hour while you enjoy a glass or 3 of chilled *vinho verde. Bom apetite!*

Manuella, a friend from the Azores who insists on authenticity, gave me a similar recipe, but used salt cod. This requires soaking in fresh water, then milk, to remove the salt. Bah! Too much like hard work! She says the Portuguese were already in Puerto Rico and were fishing the Grande Banks well before either Columbus or Cabot "discovered" the New World. As commented Simeon, Debbie's Inuit nemesis:

"What's the big deal? We already knew Hudson's Bay was there, long before you kablunas* *discovered it."*

**kabluna* means white man in Inuktitut.

A nutcracker can be used to grip recalcitrant screw tops to undo them.

Moussaka

This dish can be made in advance, and keeps for some days. The drawback is the pots and dishes required to make it. My son learned it in Albania, where it's a staple for almost every meal!

Requirements:

5 large eggplants	2 potatoes
$1^{1}/_{2}$ lb minced lamb	2 onions
1 x 10oz tin diced tomatoes	6 cloves garlic
1 x 6oz tin tomato paste	salt & pepper to taste
2 glasses red wine	olive oil
$^{1}/_{2}$ cinnamon stick	1 bay leaf
$3^{1}/_{2}$ cups milk	4oz butter
1 cup flour	2 shakes nutmeg
2 egg yolks	$^{1}/_{2}$ cup sharp cheese

Instructions:

Peel eggplant, slice to $^{1}/_{2}$ inch thick, salt liberally and drain in colander for an hour. Rinse, squeeze out excess moisture, fry in hot oil to golden brown. Set aside to drain oil. In same pan, sauté chopped onions and garlic until translucent. Set aside to drain oil. Fry ground lamb until browned and crumbly, adding tomato paste gradually. Add and reduce 1 glass red wine, drink the other. Add tomatoes, grated cinnamon, salt, pepper. Simmer until almost liquid free. Boil, drain and slice 2 potatoes to cover oiled base of baking dish, then alternate layers eggplant and meat. Meanwhile, in double boiler, melt butter, whisk in flour slowly to paste, add milk gradually, bring to boil and keep stirring as it thickens, then whisk in egg yolks, salt, pepper, nutmeg and grated cheese. Pour over top of baking dish, sprinkle with grated cheese and bake at 350°F for an hour. Rest for 10 mins.

Beef Prices

In 1969, the maximum price paid for steers, of 600lb weight and up, was 9c per lb live weight: in 2016 it is $1.20.

Sadza

The staple diet of the maShona *people of Zimbabwe is* sadza, *a very stiff porridge of grits, seasoned with a little salt. It is eaten from a common pot, using only the right hand. It takes not a little skill to pluck a bite-sized lump from the pot, roll it into a ball, then impress a well into it to receive the* chisheyu *or relish that one collects, all with the same hand from a separate pot.*

Requirements:

4 cups water   2 tsp salt

1 lb corn meal

Instructions:

Put about $^3/_4$ of the water in a large pot, add the salt and bring to the boil. Make a thick paste with the remaining water and about $^2/_3$ of the cornmeal. Slowly stir the paste into the boiling water, turn down the heat and continue stirring as it simmers for 5 minutes, then slowly shake in more cornmeal until it is almost un-stirable. Set aside to cool until hot, but not uncomfortably so, to the touch.

On the mine at Chakari, the miners took cold sadza in their lunch pails. The standing joke was that a miner's sandwich was two slices of cold sadza, with a slice of cold sadza between.

One mine captain was Alex, a huge maShona, who was friendly with the Resident Geologist, Len, a diminutive Ndebele. When they went drinking together, it was Len who talked them into trouble, (usually over his radical politics) and Alex who bashed their way out.

The partnership came very close to a gruesome end when an inebriated Len suggested to a ruling party stalwart where he should stick the AK47 with which he was endeavouring to garner their votes.

Brass Polish

Worcestershire sauce is a good polish for brass.
It isn't!
I've tried it, but it was my grandmother's writing, so it must be right.

Chisheyu

This was commonly served by local peasant farmers in the Mtoko-Mudzi area during the civil war when I was a conscript. On routine patrols through more remote areas of the tribal reservations, at every farmstead we'd be fêted and fed: to refuse was considered bad manners. You can imagine a 10 mile patrol, eating at every dusty little farm every 500 yards! The askari* were ecstatic; I was bloated.*

* askari is Swahili meaning "other ranks", who were our local militia

Requirements:

1 bunch spinach	1 or 2 tomatoes
1 cup chicken stock	1 banana pepper
$^1/_4$ cup crunchy peanut butter	1 onion

Instructions:

Shred and steam spinach, add tomato, pepper and onions, simmer and stir about 5 minutes. Meanwhile thin peanut butter with a little chicken stock then stir into vegetables. Continue heating and stirring to a creamy paste. Serve with sadza.

At one village plagued with baboons raiding the crops, I deployed our patrol to drive the troop of simians towards Sergeant Swando and myself beside a huge granite kopje, *backed by an enthusiastic crowd of spectators. As our best marksman, Swando fired first: a fine shot that had the victim emulate a rogue from a spaghetti western, as it cascaded down the cliff. His was the last shot, for the villagers surged forward, to grab, flay, gut and dismember the carcass into a massive stew pot with loads of vegetables.*

Invited to the festivities, I declined, but Sergeant Swando accepted on behalf of himself and his platoon.

Alas, I did not obtain the recipe.

Helpful Hint

My physician recommended that I limit my alcoholic intake to vintage Haut-Medoc wine, and 15 year old Single Malt whisky; because I'd never be able to afford enough to do me any real harm.

"Alas, I did not obtain the recipe."

Bobotie

A traditional South African recipe, originally from Malaysia, and contributed by who knows who, on a scribbled barely legible card. It is delicious, if you can get over the concept of curried meat with custard!

Requirements:

basic stew	topping
plenty garlic, and some	4 thick slices bread
salt to taste	$1/_2$ cup milk
2 tblsp apricot jam	1 tblsp sugar
1 apple, grated	$1/_4$ cup vinegar
a splash of oil	
1 large onion, chopped	custard
2 tblsp curry powder	4 cups milk
2 tblsp chutney	3 eggs
1 carrot, grated	parsley chopped fine
2 bay leaves	$1/_2$ tsp salt
2 lb ground beef	pepper

Instructions:

In a flat pan soak 4 slices of bread in milk-sugar-vinegar mixture. In a skillet, fry ground beef in a little oil until brown and crumbly. Add garlic and onion, simmer until browned, then add all other ingredients and simmer until carrot is tender. Drain, dump into oven pan and pack flat. Squeeze liquid from soaked bread; cover packed meat with bread. Beat custard ingredients together vigorously and pour over bread. Bake at 350°F for 1 hour.

When I first made this, Debbie didn't believe I meant to put in any custard, so she would not even taste it; until Charlie, her parrot, tried it and didn't die; so she tasted and enjoyed some. The name on Charlie's cage was Mangy Charlie, her mistranslation of Charlemagne.

If at first you don't succeed, break out the gin.

Boerewors

Nothing says: "South Africa" as loud and clear as a coil of boerewors (farmer's sausage) sizzling on the braai *(or barbeque for the uninitiated). One taste and you'll be hooked.*

Requirements:

10 lb ground regular beef	15 feet sausage skins
4 lb ground regular pork	1 tblsp allspice
1 tblsp ground cloves	1 tblsp black pepper
1 tsp grated nutmeg	1 tblsp thyme
1 oz salt	1 oz garlic salt
1 oz celery salt	$^1/_2$ lb ground coriander

Instructions:

Soak sausage skins in cold water overnight to soften and make them easy to work. Thoroughly mix spices and salts, grinding them together if necessary. Work spice/salt mixture into the meats and mix thoroughly. Pack into skins using a sausage nozzle on mincing machine. Do not twist off into links, but rather make a coil of about $2^1/_2$ feet of sausage, then twist off and start next coil. Coil would be about a foot across. This will fill your freezer.

Let *wors* stand in fridge for a day or two, so spices can spread their flavour into the meat.

When cooking boerewors, *use charcoal rather than a gas-fired barbeque, and use hardwood lump charcoal, not briquettes. It is necessary to have regular, rather than lean or extra lean ground meat, because these sausages are for cooking on a* braai. *Some like to prick* wors *before grilling, but it is better to leave it unpricked, allowing the juices to permeate the meat thoroughly. Allow flames to die down completely, then place the coil on the grill. Some fat will drip off, causing a bit of a flare up. Douse the flames with a shaken bottle of beer: souse the cook with an unshaken beer or three!*

Bee stings
To relieve a bee sting, slap on a slice of raw onion.

Biltong

As jerky is to North America, so biltong *is to southern Africa. In Zimbabwe, the maShona call it* chimkuyu, *but it is the same thing. To us from the old country, jerky is a poor relative, hardly worth wasting energy to chew it. In Brazil they make two similar dried meat products,* carne-de-sol *and* charque, *the former being like a beef ham, and considerably less salted than the latter. Both are an 'acquired taste'. The* Basileiros *cook both kinds, whereas* biltong *is eaten as is.*

Requirements:

1 beef eye of round	1 tsp celery salt
1 oz coarse black pepper	1 tsp garlic salt
2 oz whole coriander	1 tsp salt
2 tblsp red wine vinegar	

Instructions:

Pour coriander into a dry skillet, and roast until light brown and smelling strongly of citrus. Do not burn. Grind coarsely and mix with pepper. Meanwhile, cut meat lengthwise into 1 inch wide strips: you should get about 5-7 from the eye. Wash with vinegar, dab dry and rub with salt mixture. Salt initiates the drying process. Tastes vary, but do not use too much. Roll in pepper-coriander mix, then hook and hang for about 4 days.

When the biltong is the right dryness for your taste, cut across the grain into $1/_8$ inch strips, and have a chew...delicious!

I started making biltong *on the rig. Needing somewhere to hang the meat, I closed off the emergency shower in my laboratory, with suitably inscribed flagging tape: "OUT of ORDER" and "DO NOT ENTER". It was the perfect environment, cool, air conditioned, fly-free, with instant water source to wash away the dripped blood. Fortunately, no-one ever needed the emergency shower, or the* biltong *would have been ruined.*

To get rid of unwanted ticks (are they ever 'wanted'?)

To get rid of unwanted ticks from yourself or a dog, put a drop of baby oil, Vaseline or 3-in-one oil on the tick (I prefer WD40).

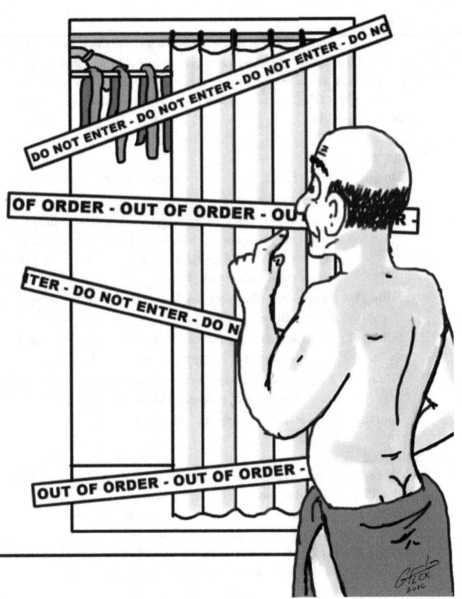

I closed off the emergency shower in my labortory,
with suitablely inscribed flagging tape...

Pyrogies

When our daughter married a Ukrainian, with a random collection of consonants without benefit of a vowel for a surname, his babka *took steps to ensure that her grandson would receive proper nourishment. With nary a Ukrainian chromosome in her DNA, our daughter is now an "ethnic food" aficionada: a dyed-in-the-wool 'Uke'.*

Requirements:

Dough   2 cups flour, $^2/_3$ cups chicken broth, 1 tblsp soft butter,

Filling A   6 medium potatoes, cut into small cubes; 2 large onions, finely chopped; enough chicken broth to cover these. Boil together for 17-20 mins. Drain the broth, which you can use for the dough. Pepper to taste.

Filling B   2 cups hot mashed potatoes; $^1/_3$ cup cheddar; salt & pepper to taste. Blend.

Filling C   2 cups hot mashed potatoes; $^1/_2$ cup real cottage cheese (not ersatz garbage); salt & pepper to taste. Blend.

Filling D   2 cups dry real cottage cheese (not plastic gloop with guar gum); 1 egg; salt & pepper, pinch of sugar. Blend.

Topping   1 onion, finely chopped, 2 tblsp butter.

Instructions:

Mix dough ingredients together until smooth and soft. Roll out thin. Cut to circles. Place 1 tsp filling on each circle, fold over and pinch edges, then crimp with fork, to seal. Drop pyrogies into boiling water. Boil 3 mins or until they float. Strain, sprinkle with onions sautéed in butter.

Making pyrogies is very much a social affair for Ukrainian women, who gather for companionship and yakking; lots of yakking.

Fitness Hint

Save money and get healthy by running home, instead of taking the bus. You can get just as fit, and save even more money, by running home instead of taking a taxi.

Borscht

On her conversion to ethnic Ukrainianism, our daughter produced borscht. *There followed a fierce argument on the proper ingredients with her brother-in-law's Filipina wife, another aficionada on all things Ukrainian. As arbiter, this is my compromise recipe.*

Requirements:

4 cups beef broth	2 onions
plenty fresh dill, and then some	1 leek
4 small beets	3 sticks celery
2 small potatoes	1 carrot
5 cloves garlic	1 small cabbage
1 small rutabaga	1 tsp marjoram
4 rashers bacon	1 parsnip
6 inches *kovbasa* sausage	splash of vinegar
1 tsp peppercorns	1 tsp allspice berries
sour cream to garnish	salt to taste

Instructions:

Dice the *kovbasa* and bacon, and fry them up in a large soup pot, then add onions and garlic and keep frying until translucent and browning, add marjoram, pepper and allspice, perhaps a bay leaf and a pinch of thyme. Finely dice all vegetables, except beets, add them, cover and simmer for 10 mins. Add broth, simmer for another 10 mins, then add grated beets and simmer again. Just before serving add chopped dill and vinegar. Garnish with sour cream and sprigs of dill.

The kovbasa *and bacon, and particularly retention of the bacon grease, is a simmering source of Filipina-African controversy; one insisting borscht should be vegetarian, the other, not. You decide.*

Desmelling Hint

To eliminate the smell of onions from your hands, rub them with baking soda or a slice of lemon.

Irish Holubtsi (Stuffed Cabbage Rolls)

Another recipe from Jeannie. She's of Irish descent, but she makes better Holubtsi than most Ukrainians, and with less fuss and bother! Our daughter also contributed an authentic alternative.

Requirements:

8 large cabbage leaves	1 lb ground beef
1 cup cooked rice	$^1/_4$ cup chopped onion
1 egg, lightly beaten	1 tsp salt
1 can mushroom soup	1 tsp pepper

Instructions:

Put cabbage leaves in the freezer for half an hour, take them out and thaw them. Core out central vein from leaves. Combine beef, rice, onion, egg, salt and pepper with 2 tblsp soup. Divide the mixture between cabbage leaves, roll them tight and secure with toothpicks. Place rolls in a shallow casserole dish, pour in remaining soup from the can, cover and bake for 45 mins at 350°F. Open the oven occasionally to baste the rolls with the soup sauce.

On my second weekend in Canada, Joe and Jeannie took me to Banff Hot Springs, in which I sat immersed, wearing a toque, while fresh snow fell on my head. The situation was so bizarre for this dumb immigrant, who was seeing snow for the first time, that I began to laugh. When Jeannie asked what was so amusing, I had to respond: "It's the first time I've been warm since I arrived in this bloody country."

Joe's contribution to the culinary arts is his martini, made by swilling out a glass with vermouth, dumping the vermouth, adding an olive, then filling the glass with crushed ice and gin or vodka; "It don't make no never-mind which". When I offered a twist of lemon as garnish he growled: "When I want a lemonade, boy, I'll ask for one."

Meat Loaf Hint

When baking meat loaf, lay strips of bacon along the bottom of the pan. Not only does it give great flavour, but it prevents sticking.

Holubtsi (Again)

My daughter's authentic alternative response to Jeannie's "Americanized" version!

Requirements:

Rolls	1 large cabbage	1 cup rice	1 onion
	$1/_4$ cup butter	$1/_2$ lb ground pork	1 egg
	Salt and pepper	4 cups chicken stock	
Sauce	2 tblsp butter	3 cloves garlic	
	2 lb can tomatoes	2 tblsp tomato paste	
	$1/_4$ cup parsley	sprig fresh thyme	
	2 tblsp flour	salt & pepper	

Instructions:

Rolls Boil cabbage in chicken stock 20 mins, drain, dry, cool on paper towels. Retain stock for rice. Boil rice in chicken stock for 10 mins. Drain, retaining stock and leave in colander to dry. In large skillet fry onion in butter until translucent. Add meat, cook gently constantly worrying with fork until crumbly, then mix in salt, pepper, rice and beaten egg and set aside to cool. Separate cabbage leaves, cut out stalk, trim spines to make easier to roll. Divide filling evenly among leaves. Fold in sides around filling, and then roll leaves from thick to thin end. Place rolls tightly in casserole dish. Half cover with retained stock. Cover tightly and bake at 375° F for 30 mins.

Sauce Melt 2 tblsp butter in skillet, stir in flour to make a roux, then as it browns, douse with $1/_2$ cup stock from above, and add all other ingredients except parsley. Simmer to reduce for 20 mins. Drain most liquid from casserole, add sauce. Bake uncovered 20 mins. Sprinkle with parsley before serving.

Add a teaspoon of glycerine to a cupful of soapsuds to make tougher bubbles for a child's clay bubble pipe.

> "After silence, that which comes nearest to expressing the inexpressible is music." Aldous Huxley

---

Kvass

While working in southwest Siberia, I was introduced to kvass *by the husband of our interpreter, Anastasia nicknamed "Nasty" (she was anything but). The drink is more popular in Russia than Coca-cola, and costs virtually nothing to make. Like the little girl with the curl, when it's good, it's very, very good; but when it's bad... At barbeques,* kvass *was served in liberal quantities, of which the kids partook freely. Their high spirits were quickly doused as they became soused and fell asleep.*

Requirements:

2 loaves dark rye bread	$2^{1}/_{2}$ gallons water
1 handful of raisins	1 oz live baker's yeast
4 cups Demerara sugar	

Instructions:

Slice bread fairly thinly, and toast as dark as possible without burning. Crumble toast into boiling water, throw in raisins, cover and stand overnight. Meanwhile, liven yeast in a separate pot with cup of sugar and some tepid water, and leave in a warm place overnight. Add yeast mixture to bread pot and leave 24 hours. Strain and squeeze through cheesecloth. Store in five two quart plastic pop bottles in fridge or root cellar, releasing pressure periodically.

I'm not sure where the raisins come in, but Nasty insisted they're necessary. Her husband, Yvan, spoke only Russian, having never left his native Barnaül, but Nasty had travelled the world, speaking fair English with a Bronx accent, which she picked up working as a stripper. When we left Siberia, they presented us each with a litre of vodka; mine in a crystal decanter, but in a regular bottle for my client, who was twenty years my junior. Doubtless they figured I deserved it more!

Moths In Drawers

To eliminate moths, put those silica dehydrating packets from shoe and pill boxes in the drawer.

Fish Amok

Cambodians eat anything that they can get a fork into, not least being deep fried tarantula, which is crunchy on the outside, gooey in the middle, like a Belgian truffle (but tasting somewhat different); barbequed frogs, stuffed with garlic and rice; ant egg soup; crispy scorpion kebabs and prahok, *a gorgonzola type cheese, made of fermented fish guts.*

Our cook was babysitting her toddler niece, who kept handling a pail full of fearsome looking live tarantulas, until Auntie Sokha scolded her; not for endangering herself, but for playing with our food.

Requirements

5 cloves garlic	1 onion
fresh green peppercorns to taste	zest of one lime
1 tsp tumeric	1 tsp coconut sugar
1 lb tilapia	1 egg
1 tsp shrimp paste, *instead of* prahok	splash of fish sauce
1 red sweet pepper	1 cup coconut milk
1 cup spinach	

salt, chili paste, fresh root ginger and lemongrass to taste

Instructions:

Mash onions, garlic, peppercorns, lime zest, lemon grass, ginger tumeric, sugar salt and chili paste in food processor, dump into hot skillet with a little oil, add shrimp paste, coconut milk, simmer for a few minutes, Add chopped fish and spinach, simmer for 3-5 minutes, then turn off heat. Mix egg and fish sauce then blend into curry on stove. Garnish with slivers of red pepper. Serve with rice cooked in coconut milk.

This is a recipe from Sokha, whose kitchen was once plagued by a young pig from the village where we were based. She chased it with a stick, threw ladles and a spade at it, shot it with a sling shot, even complained to the owner: all to no avail. Finally, we ate it, which caused a wail of anguish from the owner, but it permanently solved the trespassing problem.

Use an eye-dropper to add colouring to cake frosting.

Lok Lak

This is the quintessential recipe of Cambodia, where I spent the final six years of my career. Sokha, the camp cook, gave me this recipe, although she speaks no English, I speak no Khmer.

Requirements

1 lb eye-of-round beef	1 bulb garlic and then some	
1 tblsp black pepper	$^1/_2$ cup flour	1 Thai chili
1 tblsp coconut sugar	$^1/_4$ cup soy sauce	1 can beer
3 green tomatoes	1 onion	1 lettuce
1 small cucumber	6 green onions	2 limes
3 sprigs basil	splash olive oil	salt to taste

Instructions:

Cut beef to $^1/_2$ inch squares. Roll it in half the crushed garlic and pepper, then marinade in beer one hour. Remove beef from beer, add soy sauce to beer. Dry beef, roll it in mixed flour and a little coconut sugar. Fry until well browned in very hot skillet with olive oil, douse with marinade, reduce to thick stew. For dipping sauce, squeeze limes into a bowl, add sugar, salt, piripiri, ground pepper and remaining garlic. Serve on a layered bed of lettuce, thinly sliced tomatoes, cucumbers and onions, garnish with green onions and basil, and an optional fried egg.

To ease silk spinning, the cocoon is dropped in boiling water. This kills the chrysalis. No problem! They are collected by the Khmer, lightly sautéed, salted, then served as a snack with beer. Delicious!

When a Khmer general took me to dinner of magnificent ethnic delicacies, I asked what one particularly tasty, but boney, dish was.

"It is dtrakut," he replied. "I don't know the English word; it's like a tree crocodile."

"Iguana?" I asked, blanching slightly.

"Yeah, that's it; a bloody great lizard."

I didn't get the recipe, but I learnt it is better not to ask what you're eating.

Never let fear or common sense hold you back.

SALADS

Sister-in-law's Spud Salad

My brother's house is like a windmill, with people flocking through all the time. Their hospitality is the stuff of legend: this is its backbone.

Requirements:

twice as many spuds as there are people, plus one.

water with a healthy squirt of chicken-in-a-bottle

2 parts vinegar, 1 part olive oil,

chopped parsley green onions

pepper salt

1 tsp mustard powder per 5 potatoes

Instructions:

Boil spuds for 18 minutes in the water and chicken-in-a-bottle, drain and immediately drench with vinaigrette made with all the other ingredients. Serve warm.

Cousin Eleanor was a piece of work. She ate an entire serving dish of this salad at Great-Uncle George's funeral. I'm not quite sure how she was related to us, and I'm certain that neither my mother nor my father were any wiser than I.

She turned up at every family funeral, and at several family weddings, uninvited. After weeping prodigiously at either service (wed or dead), she was always first in line for goodies afterwards. She'd arrive with a large purse ("like a bloody cabin trunk" my brother observed) into which she'd freeload as many cookies and other dainties as it would hold. Shocked when she first encountered the phenomenon, my wife accosted her with the question:

"Can I help you?"

"Oh, no! I can manage." Cousin Eleanor replied coolly, continuing to empty a plate into her portmanteau-sized purse.

Remedy For Tape Worm

To rid yourself of a tape worm, nail it to a tree and run.

Short Salads

You don't have to be a rocket surgeon to make decent salads; you don't have to be a slave either. The essence is taste, colour and texture, taking care never to kill anyone.

Bean salad Mix together equal parts of red kidney beans, chick peas and lightly boiled green runner beans. Add a vinaigrette of 3 parts olive oil, 1 part vinegar, juice and zest of a lime, plus some chopped green onions and parsley, and salt and pepper to taste. Different coloured kidney beans adds a neat touch.

Cucumber Peel and thinly slice a cucumber. Sprinkle with salt and chopped dill. Leave until cucumber is floppy. Keeps 3 days.

Tomato Place 3 tomatoes in a deep dish; pour on boiling water; leave immersed for a minute. The skin will slide off with a sharp knife. Slice the tomatoes; arrange the slices in overlapping circles in a shallow salad dish, sprinkle with chopped green onions, salt and pepper, and a tablespoon or two of olive oil.

Israeli Coarsely chop an onion, a stick of celery, a green and a red pepper. Salt and pepper, add a handful of black olives (Kalamata are my favourite) and a generous dollop of olive oil.
Why we call this Israeli, I've no idea

Lebanese Mix equal parts stoned Medjool dates, olives, almonds and diced sharp cheese. Toss in chopped green onions and iceberg lettuce with a vinaigrette of lemon juice, olive oil, salt, pepper and a dash of balsamic vinegar.

My old boss, George, who hailed from the Lebanon, often built one of these for us on the mine on a Sunday morning. He served it with cold potatoes, boiled in their jackets and slices of salami and ham.

Hint To Help You To See Darning!
When darning a sock at night, use a flashlight as the darner.

GLOSSARY

WORD	MEANING	ORIGIN
achar	see atjar, pickled vegetable relish	India
airag	fermented mare's milk (it tastes like it sounds)	Mongolia
al dente	cooked to offer slight resistance to the teeth	Italy
amok	curry, cooked in coconut milk	Cambodia
arkhi	liquor from distilling fermented mares milk	Mongolia
atjar	see achar, pickled vegetable relish	India
au gratin	grilled with breadcrumbs on top, now topped by cheese	France
au jus	literally "with juice".	France
bacalhau	cod	Portugal
baguette	long thin bread loaf	France
béchamel	thick flour and milk sauce	France
beignet	sugared doughnut (but not quite)	France
berry sugar	finer granulated sugar, see castor sugar	
biltong	dried beef	S. Africa
biscuit	Brit-speak for cookie, Ameri-speak for scone	
bobotie	curry stew	S. Africa
boerewors	farmers' sausage	S. Africa
borscht	beet soup	Ukraine
bouquet garni	bunch of herbs, tied together or in muslin baggie	France
braai, braaivleis	Barbecue, literally 'grill' or 'grill meat'	S. Africa
brochette	see souvlaki	France
brown sugar	see molasses sugar	
café-de-Paris butter	garlic butter	France
capsicum	Aussie-speak for sweet bell peppers	Australia

carbonnade Flamande	Flemish beef stew with beer	Belgium
carne-de-sol	salted beef 'ham'	Brazil
cassonade	see Demerara sugar	France
castor sugar	finer granulated sugar, see berry sugar	
charque	salted dried beef	Brazil
chicken-in-a-bottle	liquid chicken stock concentrate	Chicken
chimkuyu	see biltong	Zimbabwe
chisheyu	relish	Zimbabwe
chorizo	farmers' sausage	Mexico
chutney	sweet vinegar pickle	India
consommé	clear soup	France
crêpe	thin, rolled pancake	France
Demerara sugar	see brown sugar	Guyana
doce de leite	caramel milk dessert	Brazil
frikadelle	see keftedes	Denmark
garnish vert-pré	typical or optimum accompanying dish	France
glacé	shiny with sugar frosting, literally "icy".	France
golden syrup	rendered and refined sweet sap of sugar cane	
haute cuisine	top-notch cooking, literally "high kitchen".	France
holubtsi	cabbage rolls	Ukraine
julienne	cut into thin, long prisms	France
kebab	see brochette	Turkey
keftedes	see frikadelle	Greece
konfyt	sugared candy from fruit	S. Africa
kovbasa	farmers' sausage	Ukraine
kvass	fermented beverage from rye bread	Russia
langues-de-chat	butter cookies	France
langues-de-chat	like butter cookie, literally "cats' tongues".	France
litre	quart	milk
lok lak	sautéed beef	Cambodia
loukoumi	Turkish delight in Greece	Greece
maître d'hôtel butter	herb, usully parsley and lemon, butter	France
maple syrup	rendered sweet sap of the maple tree	

mebos	minced dried fruit	S. Africa
meilies	green corn on the cob	S. Africa
melba toast	thinly sliced oven dried baguette	Australia
meringue	sweetened baked egg white	France
molasses sugar	see Demerara sugar	
muffin	similar to a scone, un-kneaded	
musgoes	leftovers	Canada
pain perdu	French toast, literally "lost bread"	France
pavlova	meringue topped with fruit	N Zealand
pyrogies	edible filled envelopes, like won ton or ravioli	Ukraine
quince	a round fruit rather like a pear	
ratatouille	vegetable stew	France
sadza	stiff corn meal porridge, grits	Zimbabwe
sambal	vegetable and fruit accompaniment for curry	India
scone	Brit-speak for biscuit	Scotland
simple syrup	sugar dissolved in water	
sosatie	see kebab	S. Africa
soufflé	fancy omelette	France
souvlaki	see sosatie	Greece
spud	potato	Eire
tot	distance between two fingers held up to a tumbler, the volume depending entirely upon which and whose two fingers and which tumbler are used, and how many tots were imbibed before.	Grandfather
vol-au-vent	light puff pastry small pie shell, literally "flies in the wind"	France

INDEX

TRUE DIRECTIONS

An affiliate of Tarcher Perigee

OUR MISSION

Tarcher Perigee's mission has always been to publish
books that contain great ideas. Why? Because:

GREAT LIVES BEGIN WITH GREAT IDEAS

At Tarcher Perigee, we recognize that many talented authors, speakers,
educators, and thought-leaders share this mission and deserve to be published –
many more than Tarcher Perigee can reasonably publish ourselves. True
Directions is ideal for authors and books that increase awareness, raise
consciousness, and inspire others to live their ideals and passions.

Like Tarcher Perigee, True Directions books are designed to do three things:
inspire, inform, and motivate.

Thus, True Directions is an ideal way for these important voices to
bring their messages of hope, healing, and help to the world.

Every book published by True Directions– whether it is non-fiction, memoir,
novel, poetry or children's book – continues Tarcher Perigee's mission to publish
works that bring positive change in the world. We invite you to join our mission.

For more information, see the True Directions website:

www.iUniverse.com/TrueDirections/SignUp

Be a part of Tarcher Perigee's community to bring positive change in this
world! See exclusive author videos, discover new and exciting books, learn
about upcoming events, connect with author blogs and websites, and more!
www.tarcherbooks.com

TRUE DIRECTIONS

AN AFFILIATE OF TARCHER PERIGEE

Printed in the United States
By Bookmasters